When were our Gospels Written?

AN ARGUMENT

BY

CONSTANTINE TISCHENDORF.

WITH

A NARRATIVE OF THE DISCOVERY

OF

THE SINAITIC MANUSCRIPT.

TRANSLATED AND PUBLISHED BY THE RELIGIOUS TRACT
SOCIETY IN LONDON, UNDER AN ARRANGEMENT
WITH THE AUTHOR.

PUBLISHED BY THE
AMERICAN TRACT SOCIETY,
150 NASSAU-STREET, NEW YORK.

CONTENTS.

TRANSLATOR'S PREFACE.

The name of Dr. Constantine Tischendorf is too well known to need any introduction to the English reader. As a critic and decipherer of ancient manuscripts he is without a rival, and to his other services in this important department of sacred literature he has added one which alone would reward the labor of a lifetime, in the discovery of the Sinaitic Manuscript, the full particulars of which are now given to the English reader for the first time in the following pages.

The original pamphlet of Dr. Tischendorf, *Wann wurden unsere Evangelien verfasst?* attracted great attention on its publication, now upwards of two years ago; but as it was written in the technical style in which German professors are accustomed to address their students and the learned classes generally, it was felt that a revision of this pamphlet, in a more popular form and adapted to general readers, would meet a want of the age. Dr. Tischendorf accordingly complied with this request, and prepared a popular version, in which the same arguments for the genuineness and authenticity of our Gospels were reproduced, but in a style more attractive to general readers, and with explanations which clear up what would otherwise be unintelligible. Of this revised and popular version of his proof of the genuineness of our Gospels the following is an accurate translation.

It may interest the reader to know that the pamphlet in its popular form has already passed through three large impressions in Germany: it also has been twice translated into French; one version of which is by Professor Sardinoux, for the Religious Book Society of Toulouse. It has also been translated into Dutch and Russian; and an Italian version is in preparation at Rome, the execution of which has been undertaken by an archbishop of the church of Rome, and with the approbation of the pope.

We have only to add that this version into English has been undertaken with the express approbation of the author, and is sent forth in the hope that, with the Divine blessing, it may be instrumental in confirming the faith of many of our English readers in the "certainty of those things in which they have been instructed." If the foundations be overthrown, what shall the righteous do? On the credibility of the four Gospels, the whole of Christianity rests as a building on its foundations. Hence it is that the Infidel and the Deist, with their unnatural ally the rationalizing Christian professor, have directed their attacks to the task of sapping these foundations. How unsuccessful as yet these repeated attempts of negative criticism have been, may be seen from the fact that the assault is repeated again and again. Infidelity, we are sure, would not waste her strength in thrice slaying the slain, or in raking away the ruins of a structure which has been demolished already. If the objections of Paulus and Eichhorn had been successful, the world would never have heard of Baur and the school of Tübingen. And again, if the Tübingen school had prevailed, there would not have been any room for the labors of such destructive critics as Volckmar of Zurich and others. The latest attack is, we are told, to be the last, until it fails, and another is prepared more threatening than the former. Thus every wave which beats against the rock of eternal truth seems to rise out of the trough caused by some receding wave, and raises its threatening crest as if it would wash away the rock. These waves of the sea are mighty, and rage terribly, but the Lord who sitteth on high is mightier. It is of the nature of truth, that the more it is tested the more sure it becomes under the trial. So it has been with the argument for the genuineness of the Gospels. The more that infidels have sought to shake the character of St. John's Gospel, the more collateral proofs have started up of the apostolic character of this Gospel. Thus, though they mean it not so, these attacks of opponents are among the means whereby fresh evidences of the certitude of the Gospels are called out. No one has contributed more to this department of Christian literature than Dr. Tischendorf. This is an age when little books on great subjects are in greater request than ever. No defence of truth can therefore be more serviceable than the following short pamphlet, in which, in a few pages, and in a clear and attractive style, the genuineness of the Gospels is traced up inductively step by step, almost, if not quite, to the days of the apostles.

The method of proof is one which is thoroughly satisfactory, and carries the convictions of the reader along with it at every step. Circumstantial evidence when complete, and when every link in the chain has been thoroughly tested, is as strong as direct testimony. This is the kind of evidence which Dr. Tischendorf brings for the genuineness of our Gospels.

By what logicians call the method of rejection, it is shown successively, that the Gospels which were admitted as canonical in the fourth century could not have been written so late as the third century after Christ. Then, in the same way, the testimony of the third century carries us up to the second. The writers, again, of the second century not only refer to the Gospels as already commonly received as parts of sacred Scripture, but also refer their origin to a date not later than the end of the first century.

The induction is thus complete, that these writings which the earliest of the apostolic fathers refer to, and quote as apostolic writings, must have had their origin in apostolic times. Thus we see, that of all theories, the most irrational is that of the Rationalists, who would have us believe that the Gospel of St. John was not written before the middle of the second century, and by a writer who palmed himself off as the Apostle John. We are at a loss to understand how the Church of the second century could have been so simple as not to detect the forgery, as it did in the case of the so-called Apocryphal Gospels. The Rationalists give us no explanation of this, but would have us believe, on grounds of pure subjective criticism, that the deity of our Lord was a development of the second and third centuries, after that the earlier Ebionite view of Jesus of Nazareth had been mixed up with the Alexandrian doctrine of the Logos: and that, as an amalgam of these two elements, the one Jewish and the other Greek, there resulted the Athanasian formula of the fourth century.

The historical proofs of Dr. Tischendorf blow to pieces this unsubstantial structure of inner or subjective criticism. No English reader of common sense will hesitate for an instant to decide to which side the scale inclines. With that reverence for facts which is our English birthright, we should set one single documentary proof like that, for instance, of the Codex Muratori, referred to in the following pages, against all the subjective criticism of the Tübingen school. Too long has Germany dreamed away her faith in the historical Christ, under the sleeping potions of these critics of the idealist school, who, with Baur at their head, only apply to theology the desolating and destructive theory of Hegel, that thought, when it projects itself outward, produces things; and that all things exist, because they seem to exist.

With such a school of metaphysics to start from, it is easy to see what the results would be when applied to historical criticism. "As with an enchanter's wand," facts which inconveniently did not square with the professor's theory were waved away into thin air, and history became a kind of phantasmagoria, a series of dissolving views. But the "magic lantern school," as they have been happily called, has been already discredited in Germany, and is not likely to gain much ground in this country. To complete their discomfiture, the labors of such textuary critics as Dr. Tischendorf are invaluable : critical proofs such as his are all the more acceptable as coming from Germany. The goodness and wisdom of God are seen in this, that as negative criticism had struck its roots deepest in German soil, so from Germany it is now receiving its deadliest blow. In nature, we know the antidote to certain poisons is found growing close beside the bane. In Corsica, for instance, the mineral springs of Orezza are considered a specific for the malaria fever produced in the plains below; so healthy German criticism has done more than any thing else to clear the air of the miasma caused by unhealthy speculation.

The results of a single discovery such as that of Tischendorf will neutralize to every unprejudiced mind all the doubts which subjective criticism has been able to raise as to the genuineness of St. John's Gospel. Thus it is that God's word is tried to the uttermost, and because so tried and found true, his servants love it. If the doubting of Thomas was overruled to the confirmation of the faith of all the Apostles, we see the reason why the subjective criticism of the Tübingen school has been allowed to sap, if it could, the evidence of the Gospel of St. John, in order that additional testimony should be brought from a convent on Mount Sinai to confirm us still more fully in "the certainty of those things in which we have been instructed."

THE TRANSLATOR.

OCTOBER, 1866.

THE DISCOVERY

OF

THE SINAITIC MANUSCRIPT.

As the conference of the Evangelical church of Germany, held at Altenburg, in the month of September, 1864, turned its attention to certain recent works on the life of Jesus, I was requested by my friends to put together a few thoughts on this important subject, and read them before the congress. . This I consented to do, and pointed out that M. Renan has taken strange liberties with the Holy Land; and that the history of the early church as well as that of the sacred text, contains abundant arguments in reply to those who deny the credibility of the gospel witnesses. My address was so favorably received by the congress, that the editor of the *Allgemeine Kirchenzeitung,* on the 3d of June last, made use of the following language: "I venture to say that no address has ever stirred our hearts like that short one of M. Tischendorf. As a critic he is here on ground on which he has no rival. When history speaks, it is the duty of philosophy to be silent."

Familiar as I am through my long studies with those facts which are best calculated to throw light on that great question which now agitates Christendom, I thought it right to publish the sketch of the subject, hasty as it was, which I had prepared at Altenburg. My work, printed in the month of March of this year, has been so favorably received, that in three weeks an edition of two thousand copies has been exhausted: a second edition was brought out in May, and translations into French and English were also prepared.

At the same time, the committee of the Religious Tract Society of Zwickau expressed a desire to circulate this pamphlet, provided it were recast and adapted for popular use. Although I had many other occupations, I could not but comply with their request, and without delay applied myself to the task of revising the pamphlet. I was glad of the opportunity of addressing in this way a class of readers whom my former writings had not reached; for, as the real results of my researches are destined to benefit the church at large, it is right that the whole community should participate in those benefits.

This popular tract, in the shape in which I now publish it, lacks, I admit, the simple and familiar style of the usual publications of the Zwickau Society; but, in spite of this fault, which the very nature of the subject renders inevitable, I venture to hope that it will be generally understood. Its chief aim is to show *that our inspired gospels most certainly take their rise from apostolic times*, and so to enable the reader to take a short but clear view of one of the most instructive and important epochs of the Christian church.

In sitting down to write a popular version of my pamphlet, the Zwickau Society also expressed a wish that I should preface it with a short account of my researches, and especially of the discovery of the Sinaitic Codex, which naturally takes an important place in my list of documentary proofs. The account of these discoveries is already before the public, but as it is possibly new to many of those who read the Zwickau publications, I yielded to the wish of the committee, having no other desire in this attempt than to build up my readers in their most holy faith.

As several literary and historical essays, written by me when a very young man, and in particular two theological prize essays, were favorably received by the public, I resolved, in 1839, to devote myself to the textual study of the New Testament, and attempted, by making use of all the acquisitions of the last three centuries, to reconstruct, if possible, the exact text as it came from the pen of the sacred writers. My first critical edition of the New Testament appeared in the autumn of 1840. But after giving this edition a final revision, I came to the conviction that to make use even of our existing materials would call for a more attentive study than they had hitherto received, and I resolved to give my leisure and abilities to a fresh examination of the original documents. For the accomplishment of this protracted and difficult enterprise, it was needful not only to undertake distant journeys, to devote much time, and to bring to the task both ability and zeal, but also to provide a large sum of money, and this—the sinews of war—was altogether wanting. The Theological Faculty of Leipzig gave me a letter of recommendation to the Saxon government; but at first without any result. M. de Falkenstein, however, on being made minister of public worship, obtained a grant for me of one hundred dollars to defray my travelling expenses, and the promise of another hundred for the following year. What was such a sum as this with which to undertake a long journey? Full of faith, however, in the proverb that "God helps those who help themselves," and that what is right must prosper, I resolved, in 1840, to set out for Paris (on the very day of the Feast of the Reformation), though I had not sufficient means to pay even for my travelling suit; and when I reached Paris I had only fifty dollars left. The other fifty had been spent on my journey.

However, I soon found men in Paris who were interested in my undertaking. I managed for some time to support myself by my pen, keeping, however, the object which had brought me to Paris steadily in view. After having explored for two years the rich libraries of this great city, not to speak of several journeys made into Holland and England, I set out in 1843 for Switzerland, and spent some time at Basle. Then passing through the south of France I made my way into Italy, passing through Florence, Venice, Modena, Milan, Verona, and Turin. In April, 1844, I pushed on to the East. Egypt and the Coptic convents of the Libyan desert, Mount Sinai in Arabia, Jerusalem, Bethlehem, and the convent of St. Saba on the shores of the Dead Sea, Nazareth and its neighborhood, Smyrna and the island of Patmos, Beyrout, Constantinople, Athens; these were the principal points of my route, and of my researches in the East. Lastly, having looked in on my way home on the libraries of Vienna and Munich, I returned to Leipzig in January, 1845.

This journey cost me five thousand dollars. You are ready to ask how the poor traveller, who set out from Leipzig with only a few unpaid bills, could procure such sums as these. I have already partly given you a clue to explain this, and will more fully account for it as we go on with the narrative. Such help as I was able to offer to fellow-travellers, a great deal of kindness in return, and, above all, that enthusiasm which does not start back from privations and sacrifices, will explain how I got on. But you are naturally more anxious to hear what those labors were to which I devoted five years of my life.

With this view I return to that edition of the New Testament of which I have spoken above. Soon after the Apostles had composed their writings, they began to be copied, and the incessant multiplication of copy upon copy went on down to the sixteenth century, when printing happily came to replace the labor of the copyist. One can easily see how many errors must inevitably have crept into writings which were so often reproduced; but it is more difficult still to understand how writers could allow themselves to bring in here and there changes not verbal only, but such as materially affect the meaning, and, what is worse still, did not shrink from cutting out a passage or inserting one.

The first editions of the Greek text, which

appeared in the sixteenth century, were based upon manuscripts which happened to be the first to come to hand. For a long time men were satisfied to reproduce and reprint these early editions. In this way there arose a disposition to claim for this text, so often reprinted, a peculiar value, without ever caring to ask whether it was an exact reproduction or not of the actual text as it came from the Apostles. But in the course of time manuscripts were discovered in the public libraries of Europe, which were a thousand years old, and on comparing them with the printed text, critics could not help seeing how widely the received text departed in many places from the text of the manuscripts. We should also here add that from the very earliest age of the Christian era the Greek text had been translated into different languages—into Latin, Syriac, Egyptian, etc. Ancient manuscripts of these versions were also brought to light, and it was impossible not to see what variation of readings there had been in the sacred text. The quotations made by the Fathers from as early as the second century, also confirmed in another way the fact of these variations. In this way it has been placed beyond doubt that the original text of the Apostles' writings, copied, recopied, and multipled during fifteen centuries, whether in Greek or Latin or in other languages, had in many passages undergone such serious modifications of meaning as to leave us in painful uncertainty as to what the Apostles had actually written.*

Learned men have again and again attempted to clear the sacred text from these extraneous elements. But we have at last hit upon a better plan even than this, which is to set aside this *textus receptus* altogether, and to construct a fresh text, derived imme-

* The late Prof. Moses Stuart, a learned biblical scholar and critic, gave this testimony to the general correctness of the present text of the Bible in the original languages: "Out of some eight hundred thousand various readings of the Bible that have been collated, about seven hundred and ninety-five thousand are of just about as much importance to the sense of the Greek and Hebrew Scriptures, as the question in English orthography is, whether the word *honour* shall be spelled with a *u* or without it. Of the remainder, some change the sense of particular passages or expressions, or omit particular words or phrases, but no one doctrine of religion is changed, not one precept is taken away, not one important fact is altered by the whole of the various readings collectively taken."

diately from the most ancient and authoritative sources. This is undoubtedly the right course to take, for in this way only can we secure a text approximating as closely as possible to that which came from the Apostles.

Now to obtain this we must first make sure of our ground by thoroughly studying the documents which we possess. Well, in completing my first critical edition of the New Testament, in 1840, I became convinced that the task, so far from completed, was little more than begun, although so many and such celebrated names are found on the list of critical editors; to mention only a few out of many: Erasmus, Robert Stephens, Beza, Mill, Wetstein, Bengel, Griesbach, Matthæi, and Scholz. This conviction led me to begin my travels. I formed the design of revising and examining with the utmost possible care, the most ancient manuscripts of the New Testament which were to be found in the libraries of Europe; and nothing seemed to me more suitable, with this end in view, than to publish separately with the greatest exactness the most important of these documents. I should thus secure the documents as the common property of Christendom, and insure their safe keeping by men of learning should the originals themselves ever happen to perish.

I extended, for this reason, my investigations to the most ancient Latin manuscripts, on account of their great importance, without passing by the Greek text of the Old Testament, which was referred to by the Apostles in preference to the original Hebrew, and which, notwithstanding its high authority, had during the lapse of two thousand years become more corrupt than that of the New Testament. I extended my researches also to the Apocryphal books of the New Testament, as the present treatise will readily show. These works bear upon the canonical books in more respects than one, and throw considerable light on Christian antiquity. The greater number of them were buried in our great libraries, and it is doubtful if any one of them has received the attention which it deserved. In the next place, I proposed to collect together all the Greek manuscripts which we possess, which are of a thousand years' antiquity, including in the list even those which do not bear on the Bible, so as to exhibit in a way never done before, when and how the different manuscripts had been written. In this way we should be better able to understand why one manuscript is to be referred to the fourth century, another to the fifth, and a third to the eighth, although they had no dates attached to determine when they were written.

Such, then, have been the various objects which I hoped to accomplish by my travels. To some, all this may seem mere learned labor: but permit me to add that the science touches on life in two important respects; to mention only two—to clear up in this way the history of the sacred text, and to recover if possible the genuine apostolic text which is the foundation of our faith—these cannot be matters of small importance. The whole of Christendom is, in fact, deeply interested in these results. Of this there can be no doubt; and the extraordinary proofs of interest that the Christian world has given me are alone a sufficient proof of this.

The literary treasures which I have sought to explore have been drawn in most cases from the convents of the East, where, for ages, the pens of industrious monks have copied the sacred writings, and collected manuscripts of all kinds. It therefore occurred to me whether it was not probable that in some recess of Greek or Coptic, Syrian or Armenian monasteries, there might be some precious manuscripts slumbering for ages in dust and darkness? And would not every sheet of parchment so found, covered with writings of the fifth, sixth, and seventh centuries, be a kind of literary treasure, and a valuable addition to our Christian literature?

These considerations have, ever since the year 1842, fired me with a strong desire to visit the East. I had just completed at the time a work which had been very favorably received in Europe, and for which I had received marks of approval from several learned bodies, and even from crowned heads.

The work I advert to was this. There lay in one of the libraries of Paris one of the most important manuscripts then known of the Greek text. This parchment manuscript, the writing of which, of the date of the fifth century, had been retouched and renewed in the seventh, and again in the ninth century, had, in the twelfth century, been submitted to a twofold process. It had been washed and pumiced, to write on it the treatises of an old father of the church of the name of Ephrem. Five centuries later, a Swiss theologian of the name of Wetstein had attempted to decipher a few traces of the original manuscript; and, later still, another theologian, Griesbach of Jena, came to try his skill on it, although the librarian assured him that it was impossible for mortal eye to rediscover a trace of a writing which had perished for six centuries. In spite of these unsuccessful attempts, the French government had recourse to powerful chemical reagents, to bring out the effaced characters. But a Leipzig theologian, who was then at Paris, was so unsuccessful in this new attempt, that he asserted that it was impossible to produce an edition of this text, as the manuscript was quite illegible. It was after all these attempts that I began, in 1841–42, to try my skill at the manuscript, and had the good fortune to decipher it completely, and even to distinguish between the dates of the different writers who had been engaged on the manuscript.

This success, which procured for me several marks of recognition and support, encouraged me to proceed. I conceived it to be my duty to complete an undertaking which had hitherto been treated as chimerical. The Saxon government came forward to support me. The king, Frederick Augustus II., and his distinguished brother, John, sent me marks of their approval; and several eminent patrons of learning at Frankfort, Geneva, Rome, and Breslau generously offered to interest themselves in my attempt.

I here pass over in silence the interesting details of my travels—my audience with the pope, Gregory XVI., in May, 1843—my intercourse with Cardinal Mezzofanti, that surprising and celebrated linguist—and I come to the result of my journey to the East. It was in April, 1844, that I embarked at Leghorn for Egypt. The desire which I felt to discover some precious remains of any manuscripts, more especially Biblical, of a date which would carry us back to the early times of Christianity, was realized beyond my expectations. It was at the foot of Mount Sinai, in the convent of St. Catherine, that I discovered the pearl of all my researches. In visiting the library of the monastery, in the month of May, 1844, I perceived in the middle of the great hall a large and wide basket full of old parchments; and the librarian, who was a man of information, told me that two heaps of papers like this, mouldered by time, had been already committed to the flames. What was my surprise to find amid this heap of papers a considerable number of sheets of a copy of the Old Testament in Greek, which seemed to me to be one of the most ancient that I had ever seen. The authorities of the convent allowed me to possess myself of a third of these parchments, or about forty-five sheets, all the more readily as they were destined for the fire. But I could not get them to yield up possession of the remainder. The too lively satisfaction which I had displayed, had aroused their suspicions as to the value of this manuscript. I transcribed a page of the text of Isaiah and

Jeremiah, and enjoined on the monks to take religious care of all such remains which might fall in their way.

On my return to Saxony there were men of learning who at once appreciated the value of the treasure which I brought back with me. I did not divulge the name of the place where I had found it, in the hopes of returning and recovering the rest of the manuscript. I handed up to the Saxon government my rich collection of oriental manuscripts in return for the payment of all my travelling expenses. I deposited in the library of the university of Leipzig, in the shape of a collection which bears my name, fifty manuscripts, some of which are very rare and interesting. I did the same with the Sinaitic fragments, to which I gave the name of Codex Frederick Augustus, in acknowledgment of the patronage given to me by the king of Saxony; and I published them in Saxony in a sumptuous edition, in which each letter and stroke was exactly reproduced by the aid of lithography.

But these home labors upon the manuscripts which I had already safely garnered, did not allow me to forget the distant treasure which I had discovered. I made use of an influential friend, who then resided at the court of the viceroy of Egypt, to carry on negotiations for procuring the rest of the manuscript. But his attempts were, unfortunately, not successful. "The monks of the convent," he wrote to me to say, "have, since your departure, learned the value of these sheets of parchment, and will not part with them at any price."

I resolved, therefore, to return to the East to copy this priceless manuscript. Having set out from Leipzig in January, 1853, I embarked at Trieste for Egypt, and in the month of February I stood, for the second time, in the convent of Sinai. This second journey was more successful even than the first, from the discoveries that I made of rare Biblical manuscripts; but I was not able to discover any further traces of the treasure of 1844. I forget: I found in a roll of papers a little fragment which, written over on both sides, contained eleven short lines of the first book of Moses, which convinced me that the manuscript originally contained the entire

Old Testament, but that the greater part had been long since destroyed.

On my return I reproduced in the first volume of a collection of ancient Christian documents the page of the Sinaitic manuscript which I had transcribed in 1844, without divulging the secret of where I had found it. I confined myself to the statement that I claimed the distinction of having discovered other documents—no matter whether published in Berlin or Oxford—as I assumed that some learned travellers who had visited the convent after me had managed to carry them off.

The question now arose how to turn to use these discoveries. Not to mention a second journey which I made to Paris in 1849, I went through Germany, Switzerland, and England, devoting several years of unceasing labor to a seventh edition of my New Testament. But I felt myself more and more urged to recommence my researches in the East. Several motives, and more especially the deep reverence of all Eastern monasteries for the emperor of Russia, led me, in the autumn of 1856, to submit to the Russian government a plan of a journey for making systematic researches in the East. This proposal only aroused a jealous and fanatical opposition in St. Petersburg. People were astonished that a foreigner and a Protestant should presume to ask the support of the emperor of the Greek and orthodox church for a mission to the East. But the good cause triumphed. The interest which my proposal excited, even within the imperial circle, inclined the emperor in my favor. It obtained his approval in the month of September, 1858, and the funds which I asked for were placed at my disposal. Three months subsequently my seventh edition of the New Testament, which had cost me three years of incessant labor, appeared, and in the commencement of January, 1859, I again set sail for the East.

I cannot here refrain from mentioning the peculiar satisfaction I had experienced a little before this. A learned Englishman, one of my friends, had been sent into the East by his government to discover and purchase old Greek manuscripts, and spared no cost in obtaining them. I had cause to fear, especially for my pearl of the convent of St. Catherine; but I heard that he had not succeeded in acquiring any thing, and had not even gone as far as Sinai; "for," as he said in his official report, "after the visit of such an antiquarian and critic as Dr. Tischendorf, I could not expect any success." I saw by this how well advised I had been to reveal to no one my secret of 1844.

By the end of the month of January I had reached the convent of Mount Sinai. The mission with which I was intrusted entitled me to expect every consideration and attention. The prior, on saluting me, expressed a wish that I might succeed in discovering fresh supports for the truth. His kind expression of good will was verified even beyond his expectations.

After having devoted a few days in turning over the manuscripts of the convent, not without alighting here and there on some precious parchment or other, I told my Bedouins, on the 4th of February, to hold themselves in readiness to set out with their dromedaries for Cairo on the 7th, when an entirely unexpected circumstance carried me at once to the goal of all my desires. On the afternoon of this day, I was taking a walk with the steward of the convent in the neighborhood, and as we returned towards sunset, he begged me to take some refreshment with him in his cell. Scarcely had he entered the room when, resuming our former subject of conversation, he said, "And I too have read a Septuagint, *i. e.*, a copy of the Greek translation made by the Seventy;" and so saying, he took down from the corner of the room a bulky kind of volume wrapped up in a red cloth, and laid it before me. I unrolled the cover, and discovered, to my great surprise, not only those very fragments which, fifteen years before, I had taken out of the basket, but also other parts of the Old Testament, the New Testament complete, and in addition, the Epistle of Barnabas and a part of the Pastor of Hermas. Full of joy, which this time I had the self-command to conceal from the steward and the rest of the community, I asked, as if in a careless way, for permission to take the manuscript into my sleeping-chamber, to look over it more at leisure. There by myself, I could give way to the transport of joy which I felt. I knew that I held in my hand the most precious Biblical treasure in existence—a document whose age and importance exceeded that of all the manuscripts which I had ever examined during twenty years' study of the subject. I cannot now, I confess, recall all the emotions which I felt in thát exciting moment, with such a diamond in my possession. Though my lamp was dim and the night cold, I sat down at once to transcribe the Epistle of Barnabas. For two centuries search has been made in vain for the original Greek of the first part of this epistle, which has been only known through a very faulty Latin translation. And yet this letter, from the end of the second down to the beginning of the fourth century, had an extensive authority, since many Christians assigned to it and to the Pastor of Hermas a place side by side with the inspired writings of the New Testament. This was the very reason why these two writings were both thus bound up with the Sinaitic Bible, the transcription of which is to be referred to the first half of the fourth century, and about the time of the first Christian emperor.

Early on the 5th of February, I called upon the steward, and asked permission to take the manuscript with me to Cairo, to have it there transcribed from cover to cover; but the prior had set out only two days before also for Cairo, on his way to Constantinople, to attend at the election of a new archbishop, and one of the monks would not give his consent to my request. What was then to be done? My plans were quickly decided. On the 7th, at sunrise, I took a hasty farewell of the monks, in hopes of reaching Cairo in time to get the prior's consent. Every mark of attention was shown me on setting out. The Russian flag was hoisted from the convent walls, while the hillsides rang with the echoes of a parting salute, and the most distinguished members of the order escorted me on my way as far as the plain.

The following Sunday I reached Cairo, where I was received with the same marks of good-will. The prior, who had not yet set out, at once gave his consent to my request, and also gave instructions to a Bedouin to go and fetch the manuscript with all speed. Mounted on his camel, in nine days he went from Cairo to Sinai and back, and on the 24th of February the priceless treasure was again in my hands. The time was now come at once boldly and without delay to set to work to a task of transcribing no less than a hundred and ten thousand lines, of which a great many were difficult to read, either on account of later corrections or through the ink having faded, and that in a climate where the thermometer, during March, April, and May, is never below 77° Fahrenheit in the shade. No one can say what this cost me in fatigue and exhaustion.

The relation in which I stood to the monastery gave me the opportunity of suggesting to the monks the thought of presenting the original to the emperor of Russia, as the natural protector of the Greek orthodox faith. The proposal was favorably entertained, but an unexpected obstacle arose to prevent its being acted upon. The new archbishop, unanimously elected during Easter week, and whose right it was to give a final decision in such matters, was not yet consecrated, or his nomination even accepted by the Sublime Porte. And while they were waiting for this double solemnity, the patriarch of Jerusalem protested so vigorously against the election, that a three months' delay must intervene before the election could be ratified and the new archbishop installed. Seeing this, I resolved to set out for Jaffa and Jerusalem.

Just at this time the grand-duke Constantine of Russia, who had taken the deepest interest in my labors, arrived at Jaffa. I accompanied him to Jerusalem. I visited the ancient libraries of the holy city, that of the monastery of Saint Saba, on the shores of the Dead sea, and then those of Beyrout, Ladikia, Smyrna, and Patmos. These fresh researches were attended with the most happy results. At the time desired I returned to Cairo; but here, instead of success, only met with a fresh disappointment. The patriarch of Jerusalem still kept up his opposition; and as he carried it to the most extreme lengths, the five representatives of the convent had to remain at Constantinople, where they sought in vain for an interview with the sultan, to press their rights. Under these circumstances, the monks of Mount Sinai, although willing to do so, were unable to carry out my suggestion.

In this embarrassing state of affairs, the archbishop and his friends entreated me to use my influence on behalf of the convent. I therefore set out at once for Constantinople, with a view of there supporting the case of the five representatives. The prince Lobanow, Russian ambassador to Turkey, received me with the greatest good-will; and as he offered me hospitality in his country-house on the shores of the Bosphorus, I was able the better to attend to the negotiations which had brought me there. But our irreconcilable enemy, the influential and obstinate patriarch of Jerusalem, still had the upper hand. The archbishop was then advised to appeal himself in person to the patriarchs, archbishops, and bishops, and this plan succeeded; for before the end of the year the right of the convent was recognized, and we gained our cause. I myself brought back the news of our success to Cairo, and with it I also brought my own special request, backed with the support of Prince Lobanow.

On the 27th of September, I returned to

Cairo. The monks and archbishops then warmly expressed their thanks for my zealous efforts in their cause; and the following day I received from them, under the form of a loan, the Sinaitic Bible, to carry it to St. Petersburg, and there to have it copied as accurately as possible.

I set out for Egypt early in October, and on the 19th of November I presented to their imperial majesties, in the Winter Palace at Tsarkoe-Selo, my rich collection of old Greek, Syriac, Coptic, Arabic, and other manuscripts, in the middle of which the Sinaitic Bible shone like a crown. I then took the opportunity of submitting to the emperor Alexander II. a proposal of making an edition of this Bible worthy of the work and of the emperor himself, and which should be regarded as one of the greatest undertakings in critical and Biblical study.

I did not feel free to accept the brilliant offers that were made to me to settle finally, or even for a few years, in the Russian capital. It was at Leipzig, therefore, at the end of three years, and after three journeys to St. Petersburg, that I was able to carry to completion the laborious task of producing a *fac-simile* copy of this codex in four folio volumes.

In the month of October, 1862, I repaired to St. Petersburg to present this edition to their majesties. The emperor, who had liberally provided for the cost, and who approved the proposal of this superb manuscript appearing on the celebration of the Millenary Jubilee of the Russian monarchy, has distributed impressions of it throughout the Christian world; which, without distinction of creed, have expressed their recognition of its value. Even the pope, in an autograph letter, has sent to the editor his congratulations and admiration. It is only a few months ago that the two most celebrated universities of England, Cambridge and Oxford, desired to show me honor by conferring on me their highest academic degree. "I would rather," said an old man, himself of the highest distinction for learning—"I would rather have discovered this Sinaitic manuscript than the Koh-i-noor of the queen of England."

But that which I think more highly of than

all these flattering distinctions is, the conviction that Providence has given to our age, in which attacks on Christianity are so common, the Sinaitic Bible, to be to us a full and clear light as to what is the word written by God, and to assist us in defending the truth by establishing its authentic form.

WHEN

WERE OUR GOSPELS WRITTEN?

CHAPTER I.

ECCLESIASTICAL TESTIMONY.

AND now what shall we say respecting the life of Jesus? What do we certainly know on this subject?

This question has been much discussed in our days. It is well known that several learned men have, quite recently, written works on the life of Jesus, purporting to prove that he whom Christianity claims as our Saviour did not really live the life that the gospels record of him. These works, which have been very freely circulated, have found a large number of readers. It may be that there are some points not yet fully understood, but this at least is undeniable, that the tendency of the works referred to is to rob the Saviour of his divine character.

But perhaps it will be said that the Deity of Christ is not an essential element of Christianity. Does there not remain to us its sublime system of morals, even though Christ were not the Son of God? To reason in this way seems to us to imply either that we have no idea at all of what Christianity is, or, which comes to the same thing, that we have an essentially wrong idea. Christianity does not, strictly speaking, rest on the moral teaching of Jesus, however sublime that is, but it rests on his person only. It is on the person of Christ that the church is founded; this is its corner-stone; it is on this the doctrines which Jesus and his apostles taught, rest as the foundation truth of all. And if we are in error in believing in the person of Christ as taught us in the gospels, then the church herself is in error, and must be given up as a deception.

The link then which unites the church to the person of Christ is so close, that to determine the nature of that Person, is to her the vital question of all. The Christian world is perfectly sure that it is so, and I need appeal to no other fact than her anxiety to know all that can be known of the life of Jesus, since the nature of his person can only be known through his life.

All the world knows that our gospels are nothing else than biographies of Christ. We must also frankly admit that we have no other source of information with respect to the life of Jesus than the sacred writings. In fact, whatever the early ages of the church report to us concerning the person of Christ from any independent source is either derived from the gospels, or is made up of a few insignificant details of no value in themselves, and sometimes drawn from hostile sources. These are the only sources from which opponents of the life of Christ, of his miraculous ministry and his divine character, draw their attacks on the credibility of the four gospels.

But it will then be said, How has it been possible to impugn the credibility of the gospels—of these books which St. Matthew and St. John, the immediate disciples and apostles of the Lord, and St. Mark and St. Luke, the friends and companions of the apostles, have written?

It is in this way: by denying that the gospels were written by the authors whose names they bear. And if you ask me, in the next place, why it is that so much stress is laid on this point, I will answer, that the testimony of direct eye-witnesses, like John and Matthew, or of men intimately connected with these eye-witnesses, like Mark and Luke, are entitled for this very reason, to be believed, and their writings to be received as trustworthy. The credibility of a writer clearly depends on the interval of time which lies between him and the events which he describes. The farther the narrator is removed from the facts which he lays before us, the more his claims to credibility are reduced in value. When a considerable space of time intervenes, the writer can only report to us what he has heard from intermediary witnesses, or read of in writers who are perhaps undeserving of credit. Now the opponents of our gospels endeavor to assign them to writers of this class who were not in a position to give a really credible testimony; to writers who only composed their narratives long after the time when Christ lived, by putting together all the loose reports which circulated about his person and work. It is in this way that they undermine the credit of the gospels, by detaching them completely from the evangelists whose names they bear.

This would certainly be a most effectual way of overturning the dignity and authority of the gospels.

There is another plan even more likely to effect the same end, and which they have not failed to have recourse to. There are men who call themselves enlightened who think that common sense is quite superior to Divine revelation, and who pretend to explain the miracles of Scripture, either by the imperfect ideas of these times, or by a certain prejudiced theory of the Old Testament, or by a sort of accommodation, according to which Jesus adapted his words and deeds to meet the hopes of the Jews, and so passed himself off among them as something greater than he really was.

This exaltation of common sense is not without its attractions for men of the world.

It is easily understood, and so, little by little, it has become our modern form of unbelief. Men have withdrawn themselves from God and Christianity, and it must be confessed that many of these empty and sonorous phrases about liberty and dignity of man have contributed not a little to this result. "Do not believe," they will tell you, "that man is born in sin and needs to be redeemed. He has a nature which is free, and which has only to be elevated to all that is beautiful and good, in order that he may properly enjoy life." Once admit this, and it is easy to see that this kind of unbelief will soon make way with the gospels, as well as the rest of the Scriptures. It will despise them as the expressions of an antiquated and bygone state of feeling, and will shake them off as cumbrous chains, as soon as it can.

The volume which appeared in Paris in 1863 and which has since made such a stir in the world, *La Vie de Jésus*, by M. Renan, is one of the fruits of this unbelief. This work has nothing in common with those that loyally and honestly inquire into the facts of the case. It is written on most arbitrary principles of its own, and is nothing else than a caricature of history from beginning to end. Can we suppose, for instance, that M. Renan seriously believes his own theory, that St. John wrote his gospel because his vanity was offended, either through jealousy of St. Peter or hatred of Judas? Or, when he accounts for the interest of the wife of Pilate in Jesus in these terms, that "she had possibly seen the fair young Galilean from some window of the palace which opened on the temple court. Or perhaps she saw him in a dream, and the blood of the innocent young man who was about to be condemned gave her the nightmare." Again, when he attempts to explain the resurrection of Lazarus by a deception of this same Lazarus, which was afterwards found out by Jesus, and by an act of extravagance of his sisters, which is excusable on account of their fanaticism. "Lazarus," M. Renan says, "yet pale with sickness, had himself wrapped up in grave-clothes, and laid in the family sepulchre."

These examples, which we could easily add to if we did not wish to avoid giving our readers unnecessary pain, seem to us sufficient to give our readers an idea of M. Renan's book; and since, in spite of all its frivolity, its historical inconsistency, and its tasteless disfigurement of facts, this production has made, even in Germany, such an impression, is it not plain, that alas! even among us, infidelity is widely diffused?—partly produced by, and partly the cause, in return, of our ignorance of the history of the Bible.

For this book of Renan's, German learning is in a certain sense responsible. The manner of handling the Bible which we have described already, and which consists in setting common sense above revelation, took its rise on the soil of Germany. M. Renan sets out with this principle, and there are not wanting learned men in Germany who endeavor to give it completeness, by supplying it with the scientific base which it wants. This leads us, quite naturally, to speak of the direct attacks against the authenticity and apostolic authority of the gospels, though, as far as this French work is concerned, it is written in too thin and superficial a style to be of much account one way or the other, and would certainly not have much effect in shaking any thinking person in his belief in the gospel, or cause him, without further inquiry, to give up the traditional view, that the gospels really came from the writers to whom the church refers them.

To know what we are to believe in this matter, we must carefully examine the proofs which our adversaries bring forward. The chief points in their case are the assertions which they make, and pretend to support by history of the second century—that the gospels did not see the light till after the end of the apostolic age. To support this point, they appeal to the testimony of the most ancient church literature. They maintain that the Christian writings composed immediately after the apostles do not show any trace of acquaintance with the gospels which we possess, and especially with that of St. John, and they conclude that the gospels could not, consequently, have been in existence.

If this assertion of theirs is well-founded—if there exists such a Christian literature as they speak of, that is, a series of works written between the end of the first century and the middle of the second, and if we do not find in these writings any reference to our gospels, then I should admit that the faith of the church, which teaches that the gospels were written during the second half of the first century, would be seriously compromised. Against such an assertion as this we could only raise one objection: we should ask if the nature and extent of the literature absolutely and inevitably required that it should refer to and quote the gospels, and whether we should be entitled, from its silence on the subject of the gospels, to claim such an inference as this?—for it is conceivable that many excellent things might have been written on the subject without any direct reference to the gospels. But what could they say if the direct contrary were clearly proved? I mean, if we were to find in works written a little after the apostolic age, direct quotations from the gospels; or if we see them treated with the greatest respect, or perhaps even already treated as canonical and sacred writings? In this case, it would be beyond doubt that our gospels were really composed in the apostolic age—

a conclusion which our opponents resist and deny with all their might.

The writer of this pamphlet, in common with many other impartial critics, is firmly convinced that a conscientious examination of the question proves precisely the very opposite to that which the adversaries of the gospel affirm; and this is especially true of the gospel of St. John, the most important of the four. To throw light on this important question, we must enter without delay on this inquiry, and ascertain as clearly as possible whether the most primitive Christian literature bears any testimony for or against our evangelists.

To do this, let us transport ourselves back to the last half of the second century, and inquire how the Christian church of that day thought of the four evangelical narratives.

The first thing which strikes us is, that in all parts of the church the four evangelists were treated as a part of holy Scripture. The church fathers of that age, belonging to many different countries, have written works in which they are very frequently quoted, and are always treated as sacred and apostolic writings.

At Lyons, where the first Christian church in Gaul was founded, the bishop Irenæus wrote, at the end of the second century, a great work on those early gnostic heresies, which arbitrarily attempted to overturn the doctrine of the church; and in combating these errors, he made a general use of the gospels. The number of the passages which he refers to is about *four hundred;* and the direct quotations from St. John alone exceed eighty.

We may say as much for the energetic and learned Tertullian, who lived at Carthage about the end of the second century. His numerous writings contain several hundred passages taken from the gospels; two hundred of these, at least, taken from St. John.

It is the same with Clement, the celebrated teacher of the catechetical school of Alexandria, in Egypt, who also lived about the end of the second century.

Add to these three testimonies a catalogue which bears the name of Muratori, its discoverer, and which enumerates the books of the

New Testament which from the first were considered canonical and sacred. This catalogue was written a little after the age of Pius II.—A. D. 142–157—about A. D. 170, and probably in Rome itself; and at the head of the list it places our four gospels. It is true that the first lines of this fragment, which refer to Matthew and Mark, have perished, but immediately after the blank the name of Luke appears as the *third*, and that of John as the *fourth;* so that, even in this remote age, we find even the order in which our evangelists follow each other thus early attested to—Matthew, Mark, Luke, and John.

Let us quote two other witnesses, one of whom carries us back to an antiquity even more remote. We here refer to the two most ancient versions made of the New Testament. One of these translations is into Syriac, and is called the Peschito; the other, in Latin, is known by the name of the Italic; and both assign the first place to the four evangelists. The canonical authority of these four gospel narratives must have been completely recognized and established in the mother church before they would have been translated into the dialect of the daughter churches, Syriac and Latin.

When are we to say that this took place? The Syriac version, which carries us as far east as to the banks of the Euphrates, is generally assigned to the end of the second century, and not without good reasons, though we have not any positive proof to offer. The Latin version had acquired, even before this period, a certain public authority. Thus the Latin translator of the great work of Irenæus, written in Greek, which we assign to the end of the second century—Tertullian, in fact, copies this translator in the quotations which he makes from Irenæus—aud Tertullian also, at the end of the same century, follow the Italic version. The estimation in which the Latin version of the gospel was then held necessarily supposes that this translation must have been made some ten or twenty years at least before this. It is then a well-established fact that already, between A. D. 150 and 200, not only were the gospels translated into Latin and Syriac, but also that their number was defined to be four only, neither more nor less; and this remarkable fact is well calculated to throw light on the question of their true age and origin. We shall return to this farther on.

Let us pause here to consider again these two great church teachers, Irenæus and Tertullian. Their testimony is decisive; and no one, even among those who deny the authenticity of St. John, is able to question it. We have here only to inquire whether their testimony is to be limited to the time only when they wrote; that is to say, whether it proves nothing more than the high consideration in which the evangelists were held at the time when they wrote. In his refutation of these false teachers, Irenæus not only refers to the four gospels with perfect confidence and with the most literal exactness, but he even remarks that there are necessarily four, neither more nor less; and in proof of this he adduces comparisons from the four quarters of the world, the four principal winds, and the four figures of the cherubim. He says that the four evangelists are the four columns of the church, which is extended over the whole world, and sees in this number four a peculiar appointment of the Creator of the world. I ask then, is such a statement consistent with the assertion that the four gospels first became of authority about the time of Irenæus, and that Christians then set up a fourth and later gospel, that of St. John, besides the other three older gospels? Are we not indeed constrained to admit that their authority was already then ancient and established, and that their number four was a matter already so undisputed that the bishop Irenæus could justify and explain it in his own peculiar way, as we have just now seen? Irenæus died in the second year of the third century; but in his youth he had sat at the feet of the aged Polycarp; and Polycarp, in his turn, had been a disciple of the evangelist St. John, and had conversed with other eyewitnesses of the gospel narrative. Irenæus, in speaking of his own personal recollections, gives us Polycarp's own account of that which he had heard from the lips of St. John and other disciples of our Lord, and expressly adds that all these words agree with Scripture. But let us hear his own words, as contained in a letter to Florinus:

"When I was yet a child, I saw thee at

Smyrna in Asia Minor, at Polycarp's house, where thou wert distinguished at court, and obtained the regard of the bishop. I can more distinctly recollect things which happened then than others more recent; for events which happened in infancy seem to grow with the mind, and to become part of ourselves; so that I can recall the very place where Polycarp used to sit and teach, his manner of speech, his mode of life, his appearance, the style of his address to the people, his frequent references to St. John and to others who had seen our Lord; how he used to repeat from memory their discourses, which he had heard from them concerning our Lord, his miracles and mode of teaching, and how, being instructed himself by those who were eye-witnesses of the word, there was in all that he said a strict agreement with the Scriptures."

This is the account which Irenæus himself gives of his connection with Polycarp, and of the truths which he had learned from him. Who will now venture to question whether this father had ever heard a word from Polycarp about the gospel of St. John? The time when Irenæus, then a young man, was known to Polycarp, who died a martyr at Smyrna about A. D. 165, could not have been later than A. D. 150; yet they would have us believe that Irenæus had not then heard a word from his master Polycarp about the gospel of St. John, when he so often recalls the discourses of this apostle. Any testimony of Polycarp in favor of the gospel refers us back to the evangelist himself; for Polycarp, in speaking to Irenæus of this gospel as a work of his master St. John, must have learned from the lips of the apostle himself whether he was its author or not. There is nothing more damaging to these doubters of the authenticity of St. John's gospel than this testimony of Polycarp; and there is no getting rid of this difficulty, unless by setting aside the genuineness of the testimony itself. This fact also becomes more striking if we consider it under another aspect. What I mean is this: those who deny the authenticity of St. John's gospel say that this gospel only appeared about A. D. 150, and that Polycarp never mentioned the gospel as such to Irenæus. But in this case, can we suppose that Irenæus would have believed in the authenticity of this gospel, a work that professed to be the most precious legacy of St. John to the Christian church, as the narrative of an eye-witness and an intimate friend of the Redeemer, and a gospel whose independent character, as regards the other three, seemed to take away something from their authority? The very fact that such a work of St. John had never once been mentioned to him by Polycarp would have at once convinced Irenæus that it was an audacious imposture. And are we to believe that Irenæus would produce such a forgery as this with which to reply to these false teachers, who themselves falsified Scripture, and appealed to apocryphal writings as if they were genuine and inspired? And are we further to suppose that he would have linked such a writing up with the other three gospels, to combine what he calls a quadruple or four-sided gospel? What a tissue of contradictions; or rather, to use the right word, of absurdities.

These arguments, as we have just stated them, are not new; they are at least found in

Irenæus. They have been stated before, but they have scarcely ever received the consideration which they deserve. For our part, we think serious and reflecting men quite right in attaching more weight to these historic proofs of Irenæus, derived from Polycarp in favor of the authenticity of St. John's gospel than to those scruples and negations of learned men of our day, who are smitten with a strange passion for doubt.

We say as much for Tertullian and his testimony. This man, who from an advocate of paganism became a powerful defender of the Christian truth, takes such a scrupulous view of the origin and worth of the four evangelists that he will allow to Mark and Luke, as apostolic men, that is, as companions and assistants of the apostles, a certain subordinate place, while he upholds the full authority of John and of Matthew, on account of their character of real apostles, chosen by the Lord himself. In his work against Marcion, (book 4, chap. 5,) Tertullian lays down the principle by which we should decide on the truth of the articles of the Christian faith, and especially of that most important one of all, the authenticity of the apostolic writings. For this, he makes the value of a testimony to depend on its antiquity, and decides that we are to hold that to be true for us which was held to be true in former ages. This appeal to antiquity leads us back to the apostles' day, and in deciding what is the authenticity of any writing which claims to be apostolic, we must refer to those churches which were planted by the apostles. I ask, then, is it creditable in any degree that this man, so sagacious, could have acted hastily and uncritically in accepting the credibility and authenticity of the four evangelists? The passages I have referred to are taken from his celebrated reply to Marcion, who, on his own authority, and in conformity with his own heretical tastes, had attacked the sacred text. Of the four gospels, Marcion had completely rejected three; and the fourth, that of St. Luke, he had modified and mutilated according to his own caprice. Tertullian, in his reply, formally appeals to the testimony of the apostolic churches in favor of the four gospels. Is such a challenge as this, in the mouth of such a man as Tertullian, to be passed by as of no weight. When he wrote his reply to Marcion, the apostle St. John had been dead only about a century. The church of Ephesus, among whom the apostle St. John had so long lived, and in which city he died, had surely time to decide the question, once for all, whether the gospel of St. John was authentic or not. It was not difficult to find out what was the judgment of the apostolic church on this question. Moreover, we must not forget that in Tertullian we have not merely a man of erudition, occupied in laying down learned theses; but a man of serious mind, to whom a question like this was one on which his faith, and with it the salvation of his soul, depended. Is it, then, likely that such a man would have given easy credence to writings like these, which concern the fundamental doctrines of Christianity—writings which distinctly claimed to be apostolic, and at which the wisdom of the world in which he had been educated professed to be offended? Now, as Tertullian asserts in express terms, that in defending the apostolic origin of the four evangelists he rests his case upon the testimony of the apostolic churches, we must be incorrigible skeptics to suspect any longer that he had thoroughly examined for himself into the origin of these gospels.

We maintain, then, that the attestations of Irenæus and Tertullian have a weight and a worth beyond the mere range of their own age. These attestations carry us up to the first four witnesses, and the evidence which they depose is in favor of these primitive times. This is the conclusion which we think we are warranted in drawing; and it is best established, not only by those more ancient witnesses above referred to and given by the writer of the list of books in the New Testament known as the Muratori catalogue, as well as the author of the Italic version, but also by the consent of the church and the uncontradicted records of the earliest times prior to those of Irenæus and Tertullian.

My reader has doubtless heard of those works called "Harmonies of the Gospels," in which the four narratives are moulded and fused into one. They sought in this way to produce a complete picture of our Lord's life, by supplementing the narrative of the one gospel by details supplied from another, and especially by interpolating the discourse of St. John between those of the other evangelists, so as to trace out in this way, step by step, the three years of the Lord's ministry. As early as A. D. 170, two learned men undertook works of this kind. One of these was Theophilus, bishop of Antioch, in Syria; and the other Tatian, a disciple of the great divine and martyr Justin. These two books are lost; but Jerome, in the fourth century, gives us some account of that of Theophilus, which he calls a combination of the four gospels into one; and Eusebius and Theodoret, in the fourth and fifth centuries, speak of that of Tatian in the same way. Tatian had given his the name of *Diatessaron*, that is, the gospel according to four. These two writers produced other works, which are still extant, and in which there are undoubted quotations from St. John's gospel, not to speak of the other three. But these *Harmonies*, which have not come down to us, are of much higher value than mere isolated quotations, and furnish a proof that at the time when they were first attempted the four gospels were regarded as a single work, in which the variety of the narratives, which sometimes amounts to a real difference, was plainly perceptible. Hence a desire arose to draw out of these differences a higher unity, and combine them as one harmonious whole. These two attempts to write a "Harmony" were made soon after the middle of the second century, whence we may certainly conclude that the gospels themselves were generally recognized and received as such for at least a long time previous.

We here pass by other testimonies, in order to say a few words on the letters of Ignatius and Polycarp, the disciples of the apostle, which carry us up to an age as early as the beginning of the second century. When the holy Ignatius, whom his master, St. John, had consecrated bishop of Ephesus, was led as a martyr to Rome, between A. D. 107 and 115, he wrote several letters while on his journey to Rome, of which we have two versions, one shorter and the other longer. We shall here refer only to the shorter, which is enough for our purpose, since its genuineness is now generally admitted. These letters contain several passages drawn more or less directly from St. Matthew and St. John. Ignatius thus writes in his letter to the Romans:

"I desire the bread of God, the bread of heaven, the bread of life, which is the flesh of Jesus Christ, the Son of God. And I desire the drink of God, the blood of Jesus Christ, who is undying love and eternal life." These words recall the sixth chapter of St. John, where it is said, "I am the bread which came down from heaven. I am the bread of life. I am the living bread. The bread that I shall give is my flesh. He that eateth my flesh and drinketh my blood hath eternal life." Verses 41, 48, 54.

In the same letter, Ignatius writes, "What would a man be profited if he should gain the whole world and lose his own soul?" words literally found in Matt. 16:26.

Let us quote another passage of his letter to the church of Smyrna, where it is said of Jesus that he was baptized by John, in order that he might fulfil all righteousness, and which exactly recalls Matt. 3:15.

The short letter of Polycarp, written a little after the death of Ignatius, about A.D. 115, bears reference, in the same way, to certain passages of St. Matthew. So when we read, "We desire to pray to God, who sees all, that he may not lead us into temptation, for the Lord has said that the spirit is willing, but the flesh is weak." See Matt. 6:13 and 26:41.

Though we do not wish to give to these references a decisive value, and though they do not exclude all doubt as to their applicability to our gospels, and more particularly to that of St. John, they nevertheless undoubtedly bear traces of such a reference; and we have thus an additional proof to offer, that our gospels were in use at the commencement of the second century.

It is certainly a fact well deserving of attention, that we find in the epistle of Polycarp a certain trace of the use of the first epistle of St. John. Polycarp writes thus: "Whosoever confesses not that Jesus Christ is come in the flesh is antichrist." Now we read these words in the first epistle of St. John 4:3: "Every spirit that confesses not that Jesus Christ is come in the flesh, is not of God; and this is that spirit of antichrist."

This passage of the epistle of John, as cited by Polycarp, about A. D. 115, is of very great importance, since, in fact, the ideas and style in this epistle and in the gospel of St. John are so like that we are compelled to refer them to the same writer. To recognize the epistle we must also recognize the gospel. The testimony of Polycarp, if we bear in mind the close relationship in which he stood to the apostle, is, as we have seen above, of such weight that there is no room left to contradict or attack the authenticity of writings supported in this way. To get rid of this testimony, writers of the skeptical school have made use of the following argument: "It is not absolutely necessary to take these words of Polycarp as a quotation from St. John. They may have been sentiments which were current in the church, and which John may have gathered up, as well as Polycarp, without pretending to have first originated them." A partisan of this school has had recourse to another means to evade the difficulty: "Can we not reverse the argument, and say that it is the author of the so-called epistles of John who quotes Polycarp?" A man must have some courage to start such an extraordinary theory as this; but there are learned men capable even of this. And even if this does not succeed, they have one expedient yet, which they do not fail to use as the last resort of all. They will say that the letter is not Polycarp's at all. It is true that Irenæus, his disciple, believed in its genuineness; but what matters that? One has always some good reasons with which to back up an audacious assertion, and to shake and overthrow, if possible, a truth which is firmly established. I cannot, however, help saying to any one who shudders at these antichristian attempts, that they are as weak as they are worthless, and my reader will soon see that it is so.

Let us now turn to one of the most worthy of Polycarp's contemporaries—I refer to Justin Martyr, who already had been highly esteemed as a writer, before his martyrdom in Rome—about A. D. 166—had made his memory precious to the church. Two of his works are taken up with a defence of Christianity. He presented these Apologies to the emperor, the first in A. D. 139, the second in A. D. 161.

One can easily see from these dates, and especially from the earlier of the two, that it is important to know whether Justin supports the use and authority of our gospels. It is well established that he made use of the first three, that of Matthew in particular; and this fact is beyond the reach of the attacks of doubt. This is the very reason why skeptics say all the more obstinately that he does not make use of St. John. We, on the contrary, without hesitation, assert the very opposite. In several passages of Justin, we cannot fail to recognize an echo of that special sentence of St. John, "The Word was made flesh." The reply which Justin puts in the mouth of John the Baptist, when interrogated by the messenger of the Sanhedrim, "I am not the Christ, but the voice of one crying," is nothing but a citation of a passage of St. John 1:20–23. The apostle cites the words of Zechariah—chap. 12:10—in such a way as they are found nowhere else; and as Justin uses the quotation in the same way, it is clear that he has borrowed them from St. John.

We also read in Justin's first Apology, A. D. 139, "Christ has said, Except ye are born again, ye cannot enter into the kingdom of God; but that it is impossible that those who are once born should enter a second time into their mother's womb and be born is clear to every one." There has been much dispute as to the meaning of this passage. For our part, we take the view that Justin was referring to John 3 and to our Lord's discourse with Nicodemus: "Verily, verily, I say unto thee, Except a man be born again, he cannot see the kingdom of God." That this passage of St. John occurred to Justin's mind is, in my judgment, indubitable on this account, that he adds in the same loose way in which he is in the habit of quoting the Old Testament, certain other words of our Lord, which, in the text of St. John, are as follows: "How can a man be born when he is old? can he enter the second time into his mother's womb, and be born?" If we are justified in assuming the use of the gospel of St. John by Justin, then the supposition that the gospel was only written about A. D. 150, and is consequently unauthentic, is proved to be an unwarranted assumption.

We can also show, in another way, that

Justin proves that the authenticity of this gospel was well established in his day. We will only refer to one. He tells us in the same apology, written A. D. 139, that the memoirs of the apostles, called evangelists, were read after the prophets every Lord's day in the assemblies of the Christians. Here we have to remark that the gospels are placed side by side with the prophets. This undoubtedly places the gospels in the ranks of canonical books, the same as the prophets were regarded in the Jewish synagogue. But who in the world would ever think that at the time of Justin the church used any other gospels than those which we now know of, and which, within a few years of the time, were heard of throughout the whole Christian world? Indeed, it contradicts all that we know of the rise and origin of the canon to suppose that at first, and up to Justin Martyr's time, Matthew, Mark, and Luke, only, had been accepted as canonical, and that John's gospel was brought in afterwards.

CHAPTER II.

THE TESTIMONY OF HERETICS AND HEATHEN DURING THE SECOND CENTURY.

OUR observations so far have almost entirely been confined to the writings of those men whom the church of the second century regarded as pillars of the faith. During the same period, however, there sprang up a literature of heretical and erroneous teachers, which, like grafts of a wild tree, threw up a rank luxuriance of strange doctrine. We can produce satisfactory testimony even from writings of this kind, that about the middle, and before the middle, of the second century, our gospels were held in the highest esteem by the church. This branch of our inquiry is as interesting on account of the insight it gives us into the opinions of these erroneous teachers as it is important on account of the information it gives us on the age and authority of our gospels. In appealing to these false teachers as testimony to the truth of the gospels, we follow no less a precedent than Irenæus, the well-known bishop of Lyons, to whom we have already referred. Irenæus makes the observation, "So well established are our gospels, that even teachers of error themselves bear testimony to them; even they rest their objections on the foundation of the gospels." Adv. Hær. III., 11, 7.

This is the judgment which the last half of the second century passes on the first half; and this first half of the second century is the very time from which the opponents of the gospel narrative draw their principal objections. Now surely a man like Irenæus, who lived only twenty years or so later than this very time, must have known this fact better than certain professors of the nineteenth century. The more respect then, that we pay to the real culture and progress of our age, the less can we esteem those learned men who only use their knowledge and acuteness to make away with history. What Irenæus affirms is fully borne out by facts. We may therefore, with all confidence, intrust ourselves to his guidance. As a fact, the replies of the early church fathers to these heretics, to which we owe all that we know about them, furnish positive proof that these false teachers admitted our gospels to be, as the church already declared them to be, canonical; and Irenæus, the bishop of Lyons, is one of the chief authorities on this subject. Next to him we should place a work, discovered about twenty years ago, of a disciple of Irenæus, by name Hippolitus, a man who lived sufficiently near the time of these erroneous teachers to be, like his master, a competent testimony on such a subject.

One of the most intelligent and able of these early heretics was Valentinus, who came from Egypt to Rome some time in the early part of the second century, and lived there about twenty years. He undertook to write a complete history of all the celestial evolutions which, in the mysterious region of those celestial forces and heavenly intelligences—which he called the pleroma—prepared the way for the coming of the only-begotten Son, and pretended to determine in this way the nature and power of that only-begotten Son. In this extravagant attempt, he did not hesitate to borrow a number of expressions and ideas, such as the Word, the Only-begotten, Life, Light, Fulness, Truth, Grace, the Redeemer, the Comforter, from the gospel of St. John, and to use them for his own purposes. There is thus such an undeniable connection between the gospel of St. John and this Valentinian scheme of doctrine, that one of two explanations only are possible: Either Valentinus has borrowed from St. John, or St. John from Valentinus. After what we have said already, the latter supposition must appear utterly incredible, and a nearer consideration of the subject only confirms this. Now when a skeptical school of our age resorts to such a hypothesis as this, it proclaims its own downfall. Irenæus, in fact, expressly declares that the Valentinians made use of St. John's gospel; and he shows us in detail how they drew from the first chapter some of their principal dogmas.

Hippolytus confirms this assertion of Irenæus. He quotes several of the sayings of our Lord as recorded by St. John, which were adopted by Valentinus. One of the most distinct references is that to John 10:8; of which Hippolytus writes: "Since the prophets and the law, according to Valentinus' doctrine, were marked by an inferior and less intelligent spirit." Valentinus quotes, in proof of this assertion, the words of the Redeemer, "All that ever came before me were thieves and robbers." Hippolytus, Philosophoumenon, VI. 35. It is easy to prove that Valentinus treated the other gospels in the same way as he did that of St. John. According to Irenæus, he supposed that the inferior spirit, whom he called the Demiurge, or maker of the world, was typified in the centurion of Capernaum, Matt. 8:9; Luke 7:8. In the daughter of Jairus, dead and raised to life, he fancied a type of his lower wisdom, Ackamoth, the mother of the Demiurge; and in the history of the woman who, for twelve years, had the issue of blood, and who was healed by the Lord, Matt. 9:20, he saw a figure of the suffering and deliverance of his twelfth Œon.

What bearing, then, has all this on our inquiry? Already, before the middle of the second century, we see that our gospels, and especially that of St. John, were held in such esteem that even a fantastic philosopher attempted to find support in the simple words of the gospels for his fanciful scheme of celestial powers, primitive intelligences, Œons, and so forth.

Besides Valentinus, we possess a learned letter written by a disciple of his, by name Ptolemy. It contains, in addition to several quotations from St. Matthew, a passage taken from the first chapter of St. John, in these words: "The apostle says that all things were made by it, and that without it was not any thing made that was made."

Another distinguished follower and companion of Valentinus, by name Heracleon, wrote an entire commentary on the gospel of St. John, several fragments of which still remain. In it he endeavors to twist the words of the gospel into agreement with the fancies of Valentinus. What must have been the esteem, then, in which this gospel was held in the second century, when a leading follower of such a fanciful and erroneous theorist as Valentinus should feel himself driven to draw up a commentary on this gospel, in order to make it support his heresy.

Valentinus and his school were not the

only writers who sought, though hostile to the church, to have the gospels on their side instead of against them. There were other sects, such as the Naassenes, so called from their possessing the spirit of the serpent (Nachash) that tempted our first parents; and the Peraticæ, a sect of enthusiasts, so called from their pretending to see into the heavenly future, who wove into their teachings many passages of St. John, as we learn from Hippolytus.

Already under Adrian, between A. D. 117 and 138, Basilides had written a long work to explain the gospels, in the same fantastic spirit as Valentinus. We can only infer this from a few fragments which remain to us. But we can say, with some degree of certainty, that he used the gospel of St. John; for Hippolytus expressly says that he used the expressions, "That was the true light which lighteth every man that cometh into the world," John 1:9; and "Mine hour is not yet come," John 2:4.

Let us not pass over another heretic of the early part of the second century, whose name has been used by those who take the contrary view. We refer to Marcion, in reply to whom Tertullian wrote the work we have above referred to. He was born at Sinope, on the shores of the Black sea; but it was at Rome that he afterwards wrote those works which brought his name into notice. It was his special effort to break the link which connects Christianity with Judaism, and for this reason he tried to get rid of every thing in the apostles' teaching which seemed to countenance Judaism. As we learn from church history that Marcion composed a canon of Scripture adapted to his own peculiar views, and that this collection contained only the gospel of St. Luke, with ten of the apostle Paul's epistles, and that he even accommodated the text of these to fit in with his notions, certain learned men have thought that this was the first collection of Holy Scripture known to the church—that his gospel was the original of that which now passes for the gospel of St. Luke, and that he was not acquainted with the gospel of St. John. We hold that all these three assertions are quite erroneous; as regards the second of the three, it is admitted on all sides to be so.

As to the third of these assumptions, of which so much has been made, that Marcion was unacquainted with St. John's gospel, the following testimony of Tertullian is decisive against it. This writer tells us of an earlier work of Marcion's, in which he made use of all the four gospels, and that to suit his own purposes he afterwards rejected all but that of St. Luke. We have not the least right to doubt this statement, since the whole of Tertullian's reply to Marcion rests on this point as on an undisputed fact.

These heretics, then, of the early church, have rendered considerable service by their testimony to the early reception of the gospels. We now pass them by to notice those open enemies of Christianity, to whom the preaching of the cross was nothing but a stumbling-block and foolishness. About the middle of the second century there was such a one in Celsus, who wrote a book full of ridicule and reproach against Christianity. The book itself has long since been lost—a fate which it well deserved; and yet, in spite of all its bitterness and scorn, it did no real damage to the young Christian church still suffering under persecution—a fact which is encouraging to us, who have to meet similar attacks in our day. It is well for us, however, that Origen has preserved several extracts from this book of Celsus. From these extracts we gather that Celsus, in attacking Christianity, made use of the gospels, and as "the writings of the disciples of Jesus," employed them to show what was believed by Christians. He notices in this way the story of the wise men coming from the East, the flight of the child Jesus into Egypt, the appearing of the dove at our Lord's baptism, his birth from a virgin, his agony in the garden, his thirst on the cross, etc. While he gathers these facts from the first three gospels, he takes even more details from the gospel of St. John; as, for example, that Jesus was asked by the Jews in the temple to do some miracle, that Jesus was known as the Word of God, that at the crucifixion blood flowed from his side. Of the accounts of the resurrection he notices that in one gospel there are two angels, and in another gospel only one is spoken of as present at the grave; to which Origen said in reply, that the one account is based on the gospels of St. Luke and St. John, the other on that of St. Matthew and St. Mark. We may, therefore, conclude that this heathen opponent of the gospel in the second century knew of the four gospels which we possess, and considered them, as we do, to be genuine apostolical writings.

CHAPTER III.

APOCRYPHAL LITERATURE.

THE same service which the early heretics and heathen opponents of Christianity render to our cause, we may get from consulting the so-called Apocrypha of the New Testament. My reader will ask, What is this Apocryphal literature? Now I can give some information on this subject, as I have paid much attention to it, and have discovered several originals in old libraries, and edited them for the first time. Sixteen years ago I wrote an essay, which obtained a prize in Holland, on the origin and worth of the apocryphal gospels. The apocryphal books are writings composed with a view of being taken up into the canon, and put on a level with the inspired books, but which were deliberately rejected by the church. They bear on their front the names of apostles, or other eminent men; but have no right to do so. These names were used by obscure writers to palm off their productions. But for what purpose were these apocryphal books written? Partly to embellish and add to, in some fanciful way of their own, Scripture narratives; partly to invent others about the Saviour, Mary, Joseph, and the apostles; and partly to support false doctrines, for which there was no support in Scripture. As these objects were decidedly pernicious, the church was fully justified in rejecting these writings.

They nevertheless contain much that is interesting and curious, and in early times, when the church was not so critical in distinguishing the true from the false, they were given a place which they did not deserve. We have already explained in what sense we shall use them: they will go to strengthen our proof of the early reception of the canonical gospels. Every thing will therefore depend upon the age of these apocryphal writings, and here we confine ourselves to two only, the Gospel of St. James, and the so-called Acts of Pilate. We think we shall be able to prove that both of these date from the early part of the second century. To begin with the Gospel of James.

In Justin Martyr's Apology, written A. D. 139, we find many details of the birth of our Lord, such as are only found in this so-called Gospel of James. Justin relates that the birth of Christ was in a grotto near Bethlehem; so we read in the apocryphal gospel. In the account of the annunciation to the Virgin Mary, Justin concludes with the words, "And thou shalt call his name Jesus;" and he adds, immediately after, "for he shall save his people from their sins." The order is the same in St. James' gospel. According to St. Matthew, these words were spoken to Joseph; while they are wholly wanting in St. Luke's gospel. We pass by other instances. But an objection may be raised. It may be said that Justin obtained his account from some other document since lost. For my part, I cannot agree with this objection. I find no references to any lost gospels; the attempts to discover them on the part of the skeptical school have not been successful; and as the materials of Justin's information lie before us in the gospel of St. James, I have no hesitation in ascribing it to that source. Not only does Origen mention this gospel of James as everywhere known about the end of the second century, but we have also about fifty manuscripts of this gospel of the date of the ninth century, and also a Syriac of the sixth century. To get rid of the inference that Justin made use of this gospel, we must lose ourselves in wild conjecture.

Now the whole of the writing called after St. James is so closely related to our gospels, that they must have been extensively known and used before the former was concocted. Matthew and Luke had declared that Mary was a virgin-mother: now there were sects who taught that there was also a son naturally born to Joseph and Mary: that the brethren of Jesus are referred to in the gospels seems to imply this. There were learned Jews who denied the meaning of the prophet's reference to the virgin, Matt. 1 : 23; and heathen and Jews also mocked at the doctrine of a son born to a virgin. These objections were raised as early as the former part of the second century, and the gospel of James was written in reply to these objections. It set forth by proving that from her birth Mary had been highly favored; that from her birth she was marked out as the virgin; and that her relationship to Joseph always stood higher than that of a mere matrimonial union. Now if this writing is assigned to the early part of the second century, the gospels of St. Matthew and St. Mark, on which it is grounded, could not have been written later than the end of the first century.

It is the same with the Acts of Pilate, with this difference only, that it rests on the gospel of St. John as well as on the other evangelists. Justin is our earliest authority for the writing which professes to have appeared under Pilate, and which adduces fresh and convincing testimony for the godhead of Christ from events before, during, and after his crucifixion. That it was a pious fraud of some Christian, neither Justin, Tertullian, nor any other ever doubted. On the contrary, Justin twice refers to it. First, he refers to it in connection with the prophecies of the crucifixion, Isa. 65 : 2; 58 : 2; Psa. 22:16–18; adding, "that this really took place, you can see from the Acts composed under Pontius Pilate;" and, in the second place, when he adduces the miraculous cures wrought by Christ, and predicted by Isaiah, Isa. 35 : 4–6, he adds, "That Jesus did these things, you may see in the Acts of Pontius Pilate." The testimony of Tertullian is even more express, Apology 21, when he says, "The doctors of the law delivered Jesus through envy to Pilate; that Pilate, yielding to the clamor of his accusers, gave him up to be crucified; that Jesus, in yielding up his breath on the cross, uttered a great cry, and at the instant, at midday, the sun was darkened; that a guard of soldiers was set at the tomb, to keep the disciples from taking away the body, for he had foretold his resurrection; that on the third day the earth suddenly shook, and that the stone before the sepulchre was rolled away, and that they found only the grave-clothes in the tomb; that the chief men in the nation spread the report that his disciples had taken away the body, but that Jesus spent forty days still in Galilee, instructing his apostles, and that after giving them the command to preach the gospel, he was taken up to heaven in a cloud." Tertullian closes this account with the words,

"Pilate, driven by his conscience to become a Christian, reported these things to Tiberius, who was then emperor."

These are the testimonies of Justin and Tertullian as to the Acts of Pilate. We have to this day several ancient Greek and Latin manuscripts of a work which corresponds with these citations, and which bears the same name as that referred to by Justin. Is it then the same which Justin and Tertullian had read?

This view of the question has been opposed in several ways. Some have maintained that these testimonies only existed in imagination, but that the writing itself, suggested by these very quotations, afterwards appeared. But this is a baseless supposition. Others think that the original has been lost, and that these are only copies of it. Is there any ground for supposing this? No. It is true that the original text has been altered in many places; and in the middle ages the Latins mixed up the title of the Acts of Pilate with that of the Acts of Nicodemus, and added a preface to it in this altered form; and lastly, side by side with the ancient Greek text, we have a recast of it comparatively modern. But, notwithstanding all this, there are decisive reasons for maintaining that the Acts of Pilate now extant contain substantially that which Justin and Tertullian had before them. Our own researches in the great libraries of Europe have led us to discover important documents to prove this. I would mention only an Egyptian manuscript, or papyrus, and a Latin manuscript, both of the fifth century. This last, though rubbed over about a thousand years ago, and written over with a new writing, is still legible by practised eyes. (Manuscripts of this kind are called palimpsests.) These two originals, one Egyptian, the other Latin, confirm the high antiquity of our Greek text, on which they were founded; for if there were versions of these Acts as early as the fifth century, the original itself must certainly be older.

Let us look at the matter a little more closely. This ancient work was very highly prized by the Christians. Justin and Tertullian are proofs of this, and Justin even appeals to it, in writing to an emperor, as to a decisive testimony. It still maintained its place of authority, as Eusebius and Epiphanius attest. The first tells us that at the beginning of the fourth century the emperor Maximin, who was hostile to Christianity, caused some pretended Acts of Pilate to be published, full of false charges and calumnies, and circulated it through the schools with the evident intention of throwing into the shade and discrediting the Acts which the Christians prized so highly. I ask then is it the least credible that this ancient Apocryphal book, so freely used up to this time, could have been so completely recast towards the end of the fourth or fifth century, as that the original disappeared, and a spurious version took its place? Such a supposition violates all probability, and also carries a contradiction on the face of it in that it implies that a work so mutilated could retain at the same time a certain real resemblance to the gospels. Such a theory can only mislead those who are entirely ignorant of the subject. We cannot class ourselves among such; we rather rely with confidence on our own conscientious examination of the documents, and our conclusion is as follows: Our Acts of

Pilate not only presuppose acquaintance with the first three gospels, but also and especially with St. John's; for if the details of the crucifixion and resurrection rest on the former, those of the trial of Christ refer to the latter. It follows from all this that as the so-called Acts of Pilate must have been compiled about the beginning of the second century, as Justin, A. D. 139, refers to them, the original gospels on which they are based, including that of St. John, must have been written in the first century.

This conclusion is so satisfactory and decisive, that we do not seek to add any thing to it from any further uses of the Apocryphal books of the New Testament.

CHAPTER IV.

TESTIMONY OF APOSTOLIC FATHERS. BARNABAS—PAPIAS.

THE testimony of the Acts of Pilate and the Book of James falls thus within the early part of the second century. We have advanced step by step from the latter to the former part of this century. Another remarkable writing of this age here meets us at this time—a writing which was put together by several remarkable men between the end of the second and the beginning of the fourth century. That it bears most decisively on the question of the authorship of the gospels we can now most confidently maintain since the discovery of the Sinaitic Bible. We here speak of the Epistle of Barnabas.

This epistle, in its style and matter, resembles that to the Hebrews. It is addressed to those Christians who, coming out of Judaism, desired to retain, under the New Testament, certain peculiarities of the Old; in the same way that the Judaizing teachers among the Galatians had acted. In opposition to such tendencies, the epistle asserts the truth that the new covenant which Christ established had abolished the old, and that the old was never more than an imperfect type and shadow of the new.

During the last two centuries, this epistle has been well known; but, unfortunately, the first four chapters were wanting in the copies of all the Greek manuscripts found in the libraries of Europe. It was only in a Latin version, and that of a very corrupt text, that the entire epistle was to be read. In this Latin version there was a passage, in the fourth chapter, which had excited peculiar attention: "Let us take care that we be not of those of whom it is written that many were called, but few chosen." This expression, "as it is written," every reader of the New Testament is familiar with already. I would ask you to read Matt. 4:1–11, where the temptation of our Lord is recorded. The weapon which our Lord used against the tempter is contained the words, "it is written;" and even the tempter uses this weapon in return, plying his temptation with the words, "it is written." It is the formula by which expressions out of Scripture are distinguished from all others, and marked out as the word of God written. The apostles, like the Saviour, often used the expression when introducing a quotation from the Old Testament. It was natural, therefore, to apply this form of expression to the apostles' writings as soon as they had been placed in the canon with the books of the Old Testament. When we find, therefore, in ancient ecclesiastical writings, quotations from the gospels introduced with this formula, "It is written," we must infer that, at the time when the expression was used, the gospels were certainly treated as of equal authority with the books of the Old Testament. As soon as they were thus placed side by side, there was a canon of the New Testament as well as of the Old; for the words which are referred to under the formula in Barnabas' epistle are found, as is well known, in Matt. 22:14, and also, 20:16. If this argument is of any weight, it follows that, at the time when the Epistle of Barnabas was written, the gospel of St.

Matthew was treated as part of holy Scripture.

But as the Epistle of Barnabas is undoubtedly of high antiquity, the fact that the formula, "It is written," is used, has been disputed by many learned men; and what gave some countenance to the doubt is this, that the first five chapters were extant only in the Latin version. They were able to say that this important expression was introduced by the Latin translator. A learned theologian, Dr. Credner, literally wrote, in the year 1832, as follows: "This disputed expression does not exist for us in the original Greek. It would have been easy for the translator to introduce the usual formula; and for internal reasons, we shall hold the genuineness of the phrase to be unproved till the contrary is proved." The decision, then, of the genuineness or not of the expression, depended upon the discovery of the original Greek text. And not long after these words of Credner were written, the original Greek text was discovered. While men were disputing in learned Germany as to whether the Latin version was to be relied on in this question or not, the original Greek text, which was to decide the question, lay hid in a Greek convent in the deserts of Arabia, among a heap of old parchments. While so much has been lost, in the course of centuries, by the tooth of time and the carelessness of ignorant monks, an invisible eye had watched over this treasure; and when it was on the point of perishing in the fire, the Lord had decreed its deliverance. In the Sinaitic Bible, the entire of this Epistle of Barnabas has been found in the original Greek. And how does this original text decide this important question? It decides that this expression, "It is written," was first prefixed to the quotation from St. Matthew, not by the Latin translator, but by the author himself of the Greek original.

Since this momentous fact has been decided in this unexpected way, it has been asked a second time whether we are entitled to draw from it such important consequences. Might not the formula, "It is written," have been applied to any other written book? That this could not be the case, our previous remarks on the use of the formula sufficiently prove. We have no right whatever to weaken the use of the expression in this particular case. But a critic of the negative school has tried to show his ingenuity in a peculiar way. In an apocryphal book called the Fourth Book of Ezra, written probably by some Jewish Christian after the destruction of Jerusalem, we read, "For many are born, but few shall be saved." This expression has a certain resemblance to the expression of St. Matthew, but it is clearly different. But a learned man has, with all seriousness, attempted to show that the words of the Saviour introduced by the expressive "It is written," in the Epistle of Barnabas, are not really taken from St. Matthew, but from this Book of Ezra, and that the writer of the epistle has substituted the one phrase for the other; and consequently that the formula, "It is written," applies to the apocryphal Book of Ezra, not to the gospel of St. Matthew. It is characteristic of Strauss, who has attempted to turn the life of Jesus into a mere fancy or cloud-picture, that he has marked with his approval this trick of conjuring away a passage in the Epistle of Barnabas. For our part, we see in it nothing more than an outcome of that anti-Christian spirit which has matured itself in the school of Renan. It is best described in the words of the Apostle to Timothy—2 Tim. 4:4—"And they shall turn away their ears from the truth, and shall be turned into fables." I think the reader will now agree with me when I say that, so long as nothing stronger than this can be adduced to weaken the force of this passage in the Epistle of Barnabas, no one can go wrong who simply holds by the truth. The above effort of misapplied ingenuity only proves what efforts must be made to get rid of the force of the passage.

We have to consider these conclusions yet more attentively. The Epistle of Barnabas does not date from later than the early part of the second century. While critics have generally been divided between assigning it to the first or second decade of the second century, the Sinaitic Bible, which has for the first time cleared up this question, has led us to throw its composition as far back as the last decade of the first century. In this venerable document, which Clement of Alexandria, at the end of the second century, reckoned as part of holy Scripture, there are several passages which refer to St. Matthew's gospel; as in chapter 9:13, when our Lord says, he was not come to call the righteous, but sinners, to repentance: the words, "to repentance," are here introduced in the Epistle of Barnabas, as well as in St. Matthew's gospel, by way of explanation, from Luke 5:32. It is very probable, also, that the remarks of Barnabas on the serpent of Moses as a type of the Saviour are founded on the well-known passage in John 3:14. It is remarkable, moreover, that Matthew 22:14 is introduced with the usual formula which marks a quotation from holy Scripture. It is clear, therefore, that at the beginning of the second century the gospel of St. Matthew was already regarded as a canonical book.

This result is all the more remarkable when we consider that St. Matthew's gospel has been considered not so much a book by itself as one of four gospels that together entered into the canon of the New Testament. The inquiries which we have made into the first three quarters of the second century have given prominence at one time to the gospel of St. Matthew, at another time to that of St. Luke and St. John; but the gospel of St. Mark has been less noticed, as it furnished fewer citations. It would not be fair to infer from this that the gospel which was alone cited, alone had any authority in the early church. Now the use which Justin makes of the Acts of Pilate proves to us that, at least as early as the end of the first century, the gospel of John must have been in use; and Justin himself, in the first half of the second century, makes frequent reference to St. John, and even more frequent to St. Matthew's gospel. Is not this of itself a sufficient proof that if, at the time when Barnabas' epistle was written, St. Matthew's gospel was considered canonical, the same must be the case with St. John? Basilides, in the reign of Adrian, 117–138, made use of St. John and St. Luke. Valentinus, about A. D. 140, makes use of St. Matthew, St. Luke, and St. John. Are not these additional proofs in our favor? Already as early as the time of Justin, the expression, "the evangel," was applied to the four gospels, so that the name of each of the four writers dropped into the background; and in the second half of the second century we find the number of the evangelists restricted to four, and the matter treated as a subject which was beyond dispute. What follows from this? It follows that no one of these gospels could have been elevated by itself to a place of authority in the canon of Scripture. The church only ventured to place them in the canon when they had been already received as the four gospels, and as such had been long prized as genuine apostolical writings.

When we further ask ourselves when this took place, we are forced to the conclusion that it must have occurred about the end of the first century. This was the time when, after the death of the aged John, those holy men who had known the Lord in the flesh, including the great apostle of the Gentiles and the early church, had thus lost a definite centre of authority. It was at this time, when the church dispersed over the world was persecuted without and distracted by error within, that she began to venerate and regard as sacred the writings which the apostles had left behind them as precious depositories of truth, as unerring records of the life of the Saviour, and as an authoritative rule of faith and practice. The right time had therefore come for enrolling their writings among the Canonical Scriptures. The separation between the church and the synagogue was now complete. Since the destruction of Jerusalem and the temple service, A. D. 70, the church had been thrown more entirely on her own resources, and stood now independent. It was a marked proof of her independence when she ventured to rank her sacred writings on a level with those of the Old Testament, which the Christian church herself prized so highly.

Do you ask in what way and by what act this was done? Certainly no learned assemblies sat to decide this question. If men like Matthew, Mark, Luke, and John, had left behind them outlines of the Lord's life, did it need any thing more than their names to make their writings of the highest value to the early church? And had not these men stood in such near relationship to the church as to make it impossible to pass off forged writings of theirs without detection? There was no gospel more difficult to be tampered with than St. John's. His gospel went forth from the midst of the circle of churches of Asia Minor, and spread thence into all the world. Was this possible if the slightest taint of suspicion had lain upon it? Suppose, on the other hand, that it first appeared elsewhere, then we may be sure that these Asiatic churches would have been the first to detect the fraud. It would have been impossible to palm upon them a spurious document as the writing of their former bishop.

We have an old tradition on the subject, which Eusebius in his Church History, 3, 24, has referred to. It says that the three gospels already extensively known were laid before St. John by his friends. He bore witness to their truth, but said that they had passed over what Jesus had done at the beginning of his public ministry. His friends then expressed a desire that he should give an account of this period which had been passed over. This narrative is substantially confirmed by the contents of St. John's gospel, a point which Eusebius has not failed to notice.

We conclude, then, that it was towards the end of the first century, and about the time of John's decease at Ephesus, that the church began to place the four gospels in the Canon. The reasons which lead us to assign this as the right date for the commencement of the Canon are of themselves sufficient; but we would not so confidently maintain this opinion if the history and literature of the entire second century, as far as we have been able to look into the subject, did not support our view of the case.

We have only one authority more to produce in our review of the earliest Christian literature. It is the testimony of Papias, who more than any other has been misrepresented by modern opponents of the gospel. The uncertainty which rests over Papias himself and his testimony does not allow us to class him in the same rank with the other testimonies we have already adduced. But such as it is, we here produce it.

We learn from Eusebius, 3, 39, that Papias wrote a work in five books, which he called a "Collection of the Sayings of the Lord." In collecting materials for this work, he preferred to lean rather on uncertain traditions than on what was written in books. He drew accordingly upon certain oral traditions which could be traced up to the apostles. His own words on these traditions are as follows: "I intend to put together what has been reported to me by the most ancient presbyters, in so far as I have been able to verify it through my own inquiries." He adds further, "Whenever I met any one who had held converse with these aged presbyters, I at once inquired of him what, according to the most trustworthy traditions, Peter or Philip, or Thomas, James, or John, or Matthew, or any other of the Lord's disciples, had said." It is not clear from these words whom he means by the most ancient. Some learned men have erroneously supposed that he referred to the apostles themselves as his authorities. It is much more likely that he refers to those venerable men who had spoken with the apostles. So Eusebius thinks, who had the whole work of Papias before him, and he distinctly says so. He records of Papias that he nowhere claims to have seen or heard the holy apostles but to have been a pupil of Aristion and of John the Presbyter, to whose testimony he generally refers. It struck Eusebius, therefore, that it was an error in Irenæus to call Papias a "disciple of John and the companion of Polycarp," a mistake which he fell into by confounding John the Presbyter with the Apostle John. This is confirmed by the wonderful tradition which Irenæus relates of the millennial reign, "out of the mouth of those elders who had seen John, the Lord's disciple." In this place, Irenæus undoubtedly distinguishes between these elders and the apostles. But inasmuch as he appeals to Papias as his authority for this tradition of a reign of a thousand years, he leaves no doubt that the elders of whom he speaks are no others than those named by Papias.

Eusebius gives us some further extracts from this work of Papias, namely, the story related to him by the daughters of Philip the deacon, of the raising to life of a dead man by their father, and that Justus Barnabas had drunk a cup of poison without receiving any hurt. Papias went on farther—we follow here the account of Eusebius—to give some detailed accounts which he professed to have received by tradition, such as "certain unknown or apocryphal parables and lessons of our Lord and others, some of which are fabulous." Of this kind is the doctrine of a millennial kingdom, which is to take place in a certain carnal sense on this earth after the general resurrection. Eusebius has not given us a delineation of this kingdom, but Irenæus has. It is as follows: "The days shall come in which vines shall grow, of which each vine shall bear ten thousand branches, each branch ten thousand clusters, each cluster ten thousand grapes, and each grape contain ten measures of wine; and when any one of the saints shall go to pluck a grape, another grape shall cry out, 'I am better; take me, and praise the Lord.' So each corn of wheat shall produce ten thousand ears, and each ear ten thousand grains," etc.

This narrative Papias professed to have received from certain elders, who in their turn received it from St. John. Eusebius remarks on this, that Papias, who was a man of very narrow understanding, as his book fully proves, must have got these opinions from misunderstanding some of the apostles' writings. He goes on to say that there are other accounts of the Lord's sayings taken from Aristion and Presbyter John to be found in Papias' book, for which he refers the curious to the book itself. Here, Eusebius says, he will close his remarks on Papias with one tradition about St. Mark. It is to this effect: "And so the Presbyter said—Mark, the interpreter of St. Peter, had written down whatever saying of Peter's he could remember, but not the sayings and deeds of Christ in order; for he was neither a disciple of the Lord, nor had he heard him, but, as we have seen above, learned these things from Peter, who was in the habit of referring to the events of the Lord's life as occasion might suggest, but never in any systematic way. Mark, in consequence, never failed to write down these remembrances as they fell from Peter's lips, and was never known to have failed in thus preserving an exact record of what Peter said."

To these extracts from Papias, Eusebius added another upon St. Matthew, as follows: "Thus far on St. Mark—as to St. Matthew,

Papias tells us that he wrote his Words of the Lord in Hebrew, and whoever could do so afterwards translated it." In this extract there is something obscure; it is doubtful whether we have rightly rendered "the words of the Lord," since what Papias has before observed upon Mark—we refer to the words, "What Christ has spoken or done"—makes it probable that we are to include under the expression both words and deeds. Now, all these traditions of the Presbyter John and of Papias rest upon the gospels of St. Matthew and St. Mark. Even if the expression, "the words of the Lord," is to be understood strictly, we are not to conclude that there was then no written record of these sayings already in existence, since neither Eusebius nor any other early writer ever supposed that these extracts of Papias stood in contradiction with the two gospels of Matthew and Mark. When, therefore, modern writers undertake to show that our gospel of Mark is not the original gospel written by St. Mark himself, but only a compilation from that original, this very theory convicts itself of being an arbitrary assumption. The theory is only too well adapted to invite a spirit of loose conjecture as to the origin of our gospels.

This is true of St. Matthew's gospel as well as of St. Mark's. The point of the extract from Papias about St. Matthew lies in this, that he says that the evangelist wrote it in Hebrew. If this assertion of Papias is well founded, the next saying of his, that "any one translated it who was able to do so," opens a wide field for supposing all manner of differences between the Hebrew original and the Greek text. This Hebrew text must have been lost very early, as not one even of the very oldest church fathers had ever seen or used it. My reader will see that I am casting a hasty glance at a very tangled and intricate question. For our part, we are fully satisfied that Papias' assertion of an original Hebrew text rests on a misunderstanding of his. To make this clear would take up too much space; we can, therefore, only give here the following brief explanation of Papias' error.

From the Epistle of St. Paul to the Galatians, we gather that thus early there was a

Judaizing party. This party spirit broke out even more fiercely after the destruction of Jerusalem. There were two parties among these Judaizers; the one the Nazarenes, and the other the Ebionites. Each of these parties used a Gospel according to St. Matthew; the one party using a Greek text, and the other party a Hebrew. That they did not scruple to tamper with the text, to suit their creed, is probable from that very sectarian spirit. The text, as we have certain means of proving, rested upon our received text of St. Matthew, with, however, occasional departures, to suit their arbitrary views. When, then, it was reported, in later times, that these Nazarenes, who were one of the earliest Christian sects, possessed a Hebrew version of Matthew, what was more natural than that some person or other thus falling in with the pretensions of this sect should say that Matthew originally was written in Hebrew, and that the Greek was only a version from it? How far these two sects differed from each other no one cared to inquire; and with such separatists as the Nazarenes, who withdrew themselves to the shores of the Dead sea, it would not have been easy to attempt it.

Jerome supports us in this clearing up of Papias' meaning. Jerome, who knew Hebrew, as other Latin and Greek fathers did not, obtained in the fourth century a copy of this Hebrew gospel of the Nazarenes, and at once asserted that he had found the Hebrew original. But when he looked more closely into the matter, he confined himself to the statement that many supposed that this Hebrew text was the original of St. Matthew's gospel. He translated it into Latin and Greek, and added a few observations of his own on it.

From these observations of Jerome, as well as from other fragments, we must conclude that this notion of Papias—in which several learned men of our day agree—that the Hebrew was the original text of St. Matthew, cannot be substantiated; but, on the contrary, this Hebrew has been drawn from the Greek text, and disfigured moreover here and there with certain arbitrary changes. The same is applicable to a Greek text of the Hebrew gospel in use among the Ebionites.

This text, from the fact that it was in Greek, was better known to the church than the Hebrew version of the Nazarenes; but it was always regarded, from the earliest times, as only another text of St. Matthew's gospel. This explains also what Papias had said about several translations of St. Matthew.

We have something more to say about Papias and his strange compilation. On the subject of his materials, he says that he sought for little help from written records. Of what records does he here speak? Is it of our gospels? This is not impossible from the expression itself, but from the whole character of his book it seems very improbable, since it seems to have been his object to supplement these with the traditions about the Saviour which were current about A. D. 130 or 140. We cannot suppose that the gospels themselves were the storehouses from which he compiled these traditions. He must have sought for them among those apocryphal writings which began to circulate from the very first. To those traditions of the apocryphal gospels he opposed his own collection of traditions, whose genuineness he pretended could, like the gospels themselves, be traced up to the Apostles.

We have seen already, from Eusebius' notice of Papias' work, what kind of traditions they were which he collected—traditions such as those about Philip the Deacon having raised the dead, or Justus Barnabas having drunk poison without receiving any hurt. A third tradition of the same kind, which he says is contained in the gospel of the Hebrews, is that of the history of a woman who was a sinner accused before Jesus. In this same book also, as we learn from Œcumenius, there is a story to the effect that the body of Judas the betrayer was so swollen, that being thrown down by a chariot in a narrow street, all his bowels gushed out. The book also contained, as we have already seen on the authority of Eusebius, certain unknown parables and doctrines of our Lord; but he does not think it worth his while to notice one of them; nor did any other church writer do so, with the exception of Irenæus (whose account of Papias' millenarian fancies we have already referred to), and Andrew of Cæsarea, in the sixth century, who notices in his Commentary on the Book of Revelation, a remark of Papias about the fallen angels. Eusebius, for his part, dismisses these accounts of Papias, about parables of our Lord, which he received by tradition, as "altogether fabulous."

Now, with all that we thus know about the truth of Papias and his book, what credit are we to attach to him as a testimony for our Gospels? Though there are men of ability here and there who have credited Papias, we cannot help taking the contrary side. Eusebius' opinion about Papias, that he was a man of very contracted mind, is proved, not only by the extracts from him we have already noticed, but also by the way in which his attempt to enrich the gospel narrative has been allowed to drop into oblivion by the entire Christian church. How we should have prized even a single parable of our Lord, if it had borne any internal marks of being genuine! But no one paid the slightest attention to this collection of Papias: the air of fable, which even Eusebius—who is himself by no means remarkable for critical acumen—exposes, throws a cloud of suspicion over the whole book.

Yet, notwithstanding all this, there are men in the present century, professing to be models of critical severity, who set up Papias as their torch-bearer in these inquiries. They have attempted to use his obscure and contradictory remarks about St. Matthew and St. Mark, to separate between the original element and the spurious additions to these gospels. This is indeed to set up Papias on a pedestal! But Papias is even more readily seized on by those who wish to overturn the credit of St. John's gospel. And why so? Papias is silent as to this gospel. This silence of Papias is advanced by Strauss, Renan, and such like opponents of the faith of the church, as a most damaging fact against the genuineness of the gospel. I rather think our readers who have measured Papias aright will not readily agree to this. Did not the motive betray itself, I should ask the reader whether producing Papias as a witness on such a question does not imply a misunderstanding of him and his book. His notices about St. Matthew and St. Mark do not change the character of his book. But they say that Papias could not have known of John's gospel, or he would have mentioned it; and that we have thus a proof that the gospel could not have been in existence, since Papias was bishop of Hierapolis, a town in the neighborhood of Ephesus, whence the gospel of St. John was sent forth; and the earliest record we have about the martyrdom of Papias sets it down about the same time as that of Polycarp, *i. e.* about A. D. 160.

Now, it is difficult to conceive a statement more utterly groundless and arbitrary than this, that the silence of Papias as to the gospel of St. John is a good proof against its genuineness. For, in the first place, any notice of John's gospel lay altogether out of the direction of Papias' researches; and, secondly, we have no right to conclude, from Eusebius' extracts out of Papias' book, that there was no reference to St. John's gospel in the entire book. The notices of St. Matthew and St. Mark which Eusebius quotes from Papias are not introduced to prove their authenticity, but only for the particular details which he mentions. It is quite possible that this writing did not contain the same kind of reference to St. John's writings, and this is all that the silence of Eusebius proves. Let us only add, that Eusebius, in his extracts from Papias, makes no reference to St. Luke's gospel. Are we, therefore, to conclude that Papias knew nothing of this gospel also? And yet we are logically bound to draw this conclusion, absurd as it is, in both cases.

We have only one point more to touch upon here. At the end of his notice of Papias, Eusebius remarks, that this writer has made use of passages taken from the first Epistle of John and the first Epistle of Peter. Does not this fact bear against us who refuse to see any force in his silence as to St. Luke, St. Paul, and the gospel of St. John? Quite the contrary. No one in the early church era doubted these writings, and so it never occurred to Eusebius to collect testimonies in their favor. But it was otherwise with the Catholic Epistles, the Apocalypse, and the Epistle to the Hebrews; and it was of importance to adduce testimonies in their favor. But it may be said this proceeding is arbitrary. No, we answer; and in favor of the justice of our point of view, we have two arguments to adduce. Eusebius only says one thing of Polycarp's letter to the Philippians—that it contains passages taken from the first Epistle of Peter; and yet the letter is full of quotations from St. Paul! He also mentions (IV. 26) that Theophilus, in his letter to his friend Autolycus, made use of the Apocalypse; and yet he does not so much as notice that these books contain a citation of a passage from the gospel of St. John, and even with the name of the apostle given. Now, the blind zeal of the adversaries of the gospel has either chosen not to see this, or has passed it over in silence.

But there is another argument which we can appeal to. Eusebius has told us that Papias made use of St. John's first Epistle. Now, there are strong reasons, as we have seen above, for concluding that the gospel and the epistle came from the same hand. The testimony, therefore, of Papias in favor of the epistle really amounts to one in favor of the gospel. It is quite possible that those critics who treat history so freely, after having set aside the greater number of St. Paul's epistles, can also treat in the same way the gospel of St. John, though unquestioned hitherto. They have done so; but in face of such prejudice, and a determination to see only from their own point of view, we have nothing more to say.

CHAPTER V.

MANUSCRIPTS AND VERSIONS OF THE SECOND CENTURY.

SUCH, then, are the weapons which we employ against an unbelieving criticism. But to complete our aim, and maintain the truth of the gospel, we must procure a new weapon, or rather, open a new arsenal of defence. It bears the name of New Testament Textual Criticism. It is not easy to make this at once clear to all readers; we must endeavor to do so.

The name denotes that branch of learning which is concerned with the originals of the sacred text. The inquiry into these originals should teach us what the Christian church in various times and in different lands has found written in those books which contain the New Testament. Thus, for instance, it should teach us what was the text used by Columba in the sixth century, by Ambrose and Augustin in the fourth, and by Cyprian and Tertullian, in their Latin copies, in the third and second century; and what the patriarch Photius in the tenth, Cyril, bishop of Jerusalem, in the fifth, Athanasius in the fourth, and Origen in the third, had before them in the Greek text. The chief end of such inquiries, however, lies in its enabling us to find out the very words and expressions which the holy apostles either wrote or dictated to their amanuenses. If the New Testament is the most sacred and precious book in the world, we should surely desire to possess the original text of each of its books in the state in which it left its author's hands, without either addition or blank, or change of any kind. I have already spoken of this in the account of my travel and researches, to which I here refer the reader.

If you ask me, then, whether any popular version, such as Luther's, does or does not contain the original text, my answer is Yes and No. I say Yes, as far as concerns your soul's salvation: all that is needful for that, you have in Luther's version. But I also say No, for this reason, that Luther made his translation from a text which needed correction in many places. For this Greek text which Luther used was no better than the received text of the sixteenth century, based on the few manuscripts then accessible. We have already told you that this text differs in many places from the oldest authorities of the fourth, fifth, and sixth centuries, and therefore must be replaced by a text which is really drawn from the oldest sources discoverable. The difficulty of finding such a text lies in this, that there is a great diversity among these texts; we have, therefore, to compare them closely together, and decide on certain points of superiority on which to prefer one text to another.

We have in this then a fixed point of the greatest importance on which we can safely take our stand: that the Latin text, called the old Italic version, as found in a certain class of manuscripts, was already in use as early as the second century. The text of the old Italic is substantially that which Tertullian, about the end of the second century, and the Latin translator of Irenæus still earlier, made use of. If we had any Greek text of the second century to compare with this old Italic version, we should then be able to arrive at the original Greek text at that time in use. We should thus be able to approach very nearly to the original text which came from the apostles' hands, since it is certain that the text of the second century must resemble more closely that of the first than any later text can be expected to do. Such a manuscript is before us in the Sinaitic copy, which more than any other is in closest agreement with the old Italic version. We do not mean that there are no other versions which agree as closely with the Sinaitic copy as the old Italic version, which the translator, who lived in North Africa, somewhere near our modern city of Algiers, had before him. For we find that the old Syriac version which has been recently found is quite as closely related as the Italic. The fathers of the Egyptian church of the second and third century, moreover, establish the trustworthiness of this Sinaitic text.

What, then, do these considerations lead us to? In the first place, they establish this—that as early as the middle of the second century our four gospels existed in a Syriac and in a Latin version. This fact proves, not only what the harmonists of the latter half of the second century also prove, that our gospels had already been received into the Canon, but they also decide that point which has been raised as to the genuineness of our present copies of St. Matthew and St. Mark's gospels. We have seen how certain critics, on the authority of certain loose expressions of Papias, have said that our present gospels are only versions of the original documents. To this supposition these two versions enter an emphatic protest. At least, at the time when these versions were produced, our present gospels of Matthew and Mark must have been considered genuine. This being settled, it is a groundless and unreasonable supposition that, about the beginning of the second century, there were two entirely different copies of St. Matthew and St. Mark in existence; for then we should have to admit that these authentic copies disappeared, leaving not a trace behind, while other spurious copies took their place, and were received everywhere instead of the genuine originals.

We have only one more inference to draw from the state of the text of these early documents, the old Greek, Syriac, and Latin copies. Although these set forth the text which was in general use about the middle of the second century, we may well suppose that before this text came into use it had a history of its own. I mean that the text passed from one hand to another, and was copied again and again, and so must have suffered from all these revisions. I can only here assert this as the result of my long experience in dealing with manuscripts, without going into details to prove that it was so. But I must here make the assertion as one of the most important results of my critical labors. If no one before me has been able to establish this point in the same way, this is owing to my fortunate discovery of the Sinaitic copy. Now if my assertion on this point has any solid base to rest upon, as I hope to make good on another occasion, we may confidently say, that by the end of the first century our four gospels were in use in the church. I here advance nothing new. For confirmation of what I say, I refer my reader to what I have already advanced, and endeavored to make clear and apparent to all.

And now I draw my argument to a close. Should it fall into the hands of learned opponents, they will doubtless say that I have left out much that is important. This seems to me to be mere trifling. It is easy for writers with a little subtlety to expose the contradictions and mistakes of certain early church fathers; and it is to meet these special pleadings that historical testimony becomes so important. A single well-established fact weighs more in the scale of good sense than the most dazzling wit, the most ingenious sophistry, with which they torture and twist the facts which occurred eighteen hundred years ago.

May my writing serve this end, to make you mistrust those novel theories upon, or rather against, the gospels, which would persuade you that the glorious details which the gospels give us of our gracious Saviour are founded on ignorance or deceit. The gospels, like the Only-Begotten of the Father, will endure as long as human nature itself, while the discoveries of this pretended wisdom must sooner or later disappear as soap-bubbles. He who has made shipwreck of his own faith and fallen away to the flesh, cannot endure to see others trusting in their Saviour. Do not, then, let yourself be disturbed by their clamor, but rather hold firmly what you have, the more others assail it. Do not think that we are dubious about the final victory of truth. For this result there is One pledged to whom the whole world is mere feebleness. All that concerns our duty is, to bear testimony to the truth, to the best of our ability, and that not for victory, but for conscience' sake.

www.ingramcontent.com/pod-product-compliance
Lightning Source LLC
LaVergne TN
LVHW021420110826
845150LV00007B/2016

* 9 7 8 1 4 2 5 5 0 9 4 1 5 *